STUDIES IN
ANTHROPOLOGICAL METHOD

General Editors
GEORGE AND LOUISE SPINDLER
Stanford University

USING HISTORICAL SOURCES IN ANTHROPOLOGY AND SOCIOLOGY

USING HISTORICAL
SOURCES IN
ANTHROPOLOGY
AND SOCIOLOGY

DAVID C. PITT
University of Waikato, New Zealand

HOLT, RINEHART AND WINSTON, INC.

New York   Chicago   San Francisco   Atlanta
Dallas   Montreal   Toronto   London   Sydney

FOREWORD

ABOUT THE SERIES

Anthropology has been, since the turn of the century, a significant influence shaping Western thought. It has brought into proper perspective the position of our culture as one of many and has challenged universalistic and absolutistic assumptions and beliefs about the proper condition of man. Anthropology has been able to make this contribution mainly through its descriptive analyses of non-Western ways of life. Only in the last decades of its comparatively short existence as a science have anthropologists developed systematic theories about human behavior in its transcultural dimensions, and only very recently have anthropological techniques of data collection and analysis become explicit and in some instances replicable.

Teachers of anthropology have been handicapped by the lack of clear, authoritative statements of how anthropologists collect and analyze relevant data. The results of fieldwork are available in the ethnographies and they can be used to demonstrate cultural diversity and integration, social control, religious behavior, marriage customs, and the like, but clear, systematic statements about how the facts are gathered and interpreted are rare in the literature readily available to students. Without this information the alert reader of anthropological literature is left uninformed about the process of our science, knowing only the results. This is an unsatisfying state of affairs for both the student and the instructor.

This series is designed to help solve this problem. Each study in the series focuses upon manageable dimensions of modern anthropological methodology. Each one demonstrates significant aspects of the processes of gathering, ordering, and interpreting data. Some are highly selected dimensions of methodology. Others are concerned with the whole range of experience involved in studying a total society. These studies are written by professional anthropologists who have done fieldwork and have made significant contributions to the science of man and his works. In them the authors explain how they go about this work and to what end. We think they will be helpful to students who want to know what processes of inquiry and ordering stand behind the formal, published results of anthropology.

ABOUT THE AUTHOR

David C. Pitt was born in New Zealand and graduated in history and anthropology from the University of New Zealand and Oxford University. At Oxford he worked for his doctorate under Professor Evans-Pritchard, the anthropologist who did so much to further the links with history. During his research he became convinced that historical documents, properly used, could become an important research tool for the social anthropologist. Professor Pitt has taught at universities in England, Canada, and New Zealand, where he is presently Head of Sociology at the University of Waikato. He has done fieldwork and historical research in Western Samoa, Malaysia, New Zealand, and Switzerland. His major theoretical interests are in problems of economic development and social change. In this field he has also worked for the United Nations, particularly on questions of Asian development. His major publications include a monograph on economic development in Samoa (Pitt 1969).

ABOUT THE BOOK

It is paradoxical but not unpredictable that, as the traditional tribesmen and folk communities the world over become industrialized and urbanized, the anthropologist, whose special interest they were, should turn to studies of contemporary modern societies as one form of adaptation and to historical documents that can give time depth to cultural change as another. Anthropologists in particular, and sociologists secondarily, have long been criticized for underplaying the diachronic dimension in their studies. The tendency has been to look at communities as ongoing processes without a past, even though, as David Pitt points out, there has been a tradition of ethnohistory in American anthropological scholarship. There is a current movement within both anthropology and sociology to turn more seriously to adaptive processes over time and the documents that make the analysis of them possible. This book provides guidelines for the use of historical data and documentary sources. It is written by a cultural anthropologist who is experienced in the use of historical sources and values their use, but who writes as an anthropologist, not as a historian. We believe that this book will be helpful not only to students of ethnohistory but also to any student whose concern is the study of social and cultural adaptation. The reader will also find that the concerns developed in this study go well beyond the mere practical aspects of the use of historical materials into broader considerations of method and theoretical approach.

The author provides in this relatively brief book a relevant coverage of the significance of history and of the documentary record, the sources of material, procedures of gaining access to and recording data, and an analysis of certain problems in the use of documentary evidence. At the end of each chapter there is a detailed guide to relevant literature on the use of historical and documentary sources. As an example of the way in which documentary sources may play a significant role in research, the author includes a description of a project that he himself carried out in Samoa on the social context of economic activity. The book concludes with a series of problems and questions intended as an aid to the student in developing useful approaches to learning about the uses of documents and the significance of historical research.

GEORGE AND LOUISE SPINDLER
General Editors

Phlox, Wisconsin, June 1971

CONTENTS

Introduction

I T IS THE PURPOSE of this book to set out the ways in which historical documents have been, or may be, of use to the cultural or social anthropologist and sociologist. I am especially interested in the ways in which the use of the documentary record may be integrated with the more traditional fieldwork and research methods in the two disciplines. In recent years there has been a growing interest, in both anthropology and sociology, in historical perspectives, an interest generated in both fields by the desire to deepen structural understanding in a world of change and dynamism. Although methodologically and theoretically estranged in many ways, the two disciplines have similar problems and possibilities in historical research.

This brief book does not pretend to be a comprehensive guide to historical methodology. There are many historians with a lifetime of research behind them who have prepared such guides more than adequately and to whom the research worker can turn. This book rather picks out some of the important steps and considerations needed before historical sources can be utilized by the cultural anthropologist or sociologist. Many of the ideas in fact have sprung from my own attempts to utilize historical data in conjunction with fieldwork and, to some extent, social surveys, particularly in Western Samoa, New Zealand, and rural Switzerland. Probably, my selection of salient points is for this reason rather subjective; hopefully, however, these locally derived experiences will illuminate more general problems.

I owe thanks to many individuals, though only I am responsible for the final product. I am particularly indebted to Professor E. Evans-Pritchard, who originally pointed me toward the borderland between anthropology and history, and Rudi Ziedins, who kindly read and commented on parts of the manuscript. I would like to thank the staff of Holt, Rinehart and Winston for much editorial assistance. As always, my family contributed much in many ways.

1

┌─────┐
│ 1 │
└─────┘

The Context of Historical Research

The Importance of the Documentary Record

METHODOLOGICALLY, the most important contribution of cultural or social anthropology to the social sciences has been the development of techniques of fieldwork, of direct and intensive participant observation in small, often isolated, communities. Sociology, especially in North America, has been most concerned with small groups, interpersonal relations, decision making, and so forth, and with developing quantitative techniques to help study these interests. In both disciplines the accent has been on the more or less directly observed present.

The reasons for this focus are complex. Some anthropologists have claimed that the shortages and quality of documents concerning preliterate Afro-Asian peoples have restricted or prevented historical analysis. Theoretical interests, especially present-oriented structural–functionalist concerns, have concentrated focus as well. The academic separation of historians and sociologists and anthropologists, isolated from one another in different intellectual subcultures (Cohn 1962, K. Thomas 1963), has also had a tremendous effect on the concerns of the respective groups of investigators.

Despite this trend, there is presently widespread use of historical research in both anthropology and sociology. This is a movement which is currently gaining in strength, partly as a reaction to the exploding mass of available documentation about all societies, even the most remote Amazon tribe.

There are many other reasons why the documentary record may assume an importance, even a critical importance. During his research the anthropologist or sociologist only sees or surveys the social structure and culture at a given restricted point in time and space. But this structure is part of a historical continuity, on the one hand, and, on the other, is intimately related to the world outside the observed segment. The documentary record provides important insights into this world which cannot be observed but which is an integral part of the

3

things which the researcher purports to understand. The present is too flat a dimension to allow the broad features of the social landscape to be seen in clear relief. That which is structurally significant is often that which lasts and is continuous. But if a time depth is necessary to understand the constant, it is more necessary to understand the changes. The present contains the illusion of stability. The changes (and in many parts of the world, these are rapid and extensive) and their present extensions or repercussions can only be understood through some historical knowledge.

More specifically, the research worker may not be able to see all the significant possibilities in the social structure at the time of his fieldwork or study. For example, the anthropological fieldworker during his stay in a village may witness most, if not all, stages in the kinship development cycle. But he is not in the same position if he is studying political institutions. He is much less likely to see even a single succession to high office, a revolution, a rebellion, or other climactic events which are the core of political life. Southwold's (1968) study of fraternal succession in Buganda illustrates well how the range of candidates, and the criteria for selection in a major dynasty, can only be discovered from the historical record.

In my work on economic development in Samoa (Pitt 1970) I discovered in the historical record a number of important economic institutions (for example, large Samoan trading companies) which were an integral part of the confrontation with the European commercial world but not present in the contemporary social structure. The fieldwork evidence cannot adequately cover such unobserved segments. The facts may have been forgotten. As likely, if the facts are important, they will have been embodied in a local history which may mold the past to suit the present (see, for example, Cunnison 1959).

A thorough knowledge of the historical record may also prevent errors in the interpretation of the present (Lipset and Hofstadter 1968:20). For example, Oscar Handlin and Stephen Thernstrom have shown how W. L. Warner misinterpreted a number of aspects of Yankee City society by relying on contemporary reports and ignoring documentary sources (Thernstrom 1964).

The historical record provides then a time depth, but equally important are the comparative insights. Most anthropologists have time to study from their fieldwork just one society; only a few study more than two or three. Such a concentration, whatever its advantages, inevitably creates a restricted viewpoint, and it has been said (see, for example, Jarvie 1964) that many anthropologists see all the problems of anthropology—or, indeed, of mankind—in terms of their one society. Jarvie (1964) has argued that largely because of this, contemporary anthropology is short on solid theory, and others (see, for example, Needham 1962) have claimed that anthropologists are living off the intellectual capital of the nineteenth century. Comparative research is increasingly important also among sociologists seeking wider perspectives and generalizations (see, for example, Wertheim 1964 and Marsh 1967).

There is another relevant problem. Although there has been a population explosion among professional social scientists and graduate students in recent years, there are still far too few people available to study, by direct observation methods, the traditional societies of the world, which are being swallowed up by the flood tides of modernization and acculturation. Scholars are being forced to look for shortcuts to salvage what they can, and historical records can play a part in this process.

Even where the researcher is mainly involved in a fieldwork study, historical methods still perform an important ancillary role. The documentary record can assume a great importance if there are serious restrictions on fieldwork liberty, for instance, if political or official factors limit investigation, or if, in the societies and subcultures under study (and there are many), rules of privacy, secrecy, or decorum cloak or disguise significant data from the most penetrating observation. Nor can observation or survey cover in detail and with accuracy every facet of the social organization. Historical documents provide an additional check. Such a check is particularly valuable in survey work, where distortions and omissions inevitably occur even when questionnaire construction, sampling, and interview technique are of a high standard.

Then, of course, there are societies, aside from those in the past, which cannot be reached by the fieldworker. For example, Western fieldworkers are generally not permitted in the communist world. The Dunns (E. Dunn and S. Dunn 1967) have shown that a huge, largely untapped repository of documentation exists for the study of Russian society.

Finally, as anthropology and sociology acquire a history and historical documents in their own right, and as the members of the profession bequeath their papers to posterity, the techniques of the historian, as Stocking (1968) has recently shown, become necessary to elucidate theoretical developments.

Models for Historical Data

More specific uses of historical materials can be quickly appreciated from even a cursory glance at the literature. This section will serve to indicate not only the importance of historical materials but also something of the theoretical context in which historical analysis has proceeded. This context is of paramount importance in the use and interpretation of historical data. No historical record is a complete chronicle of past events or facts. The process of selectivity depends on the kinds of models or theories with which the researcher works.

The founding fathers of the nineteenth century used historical documents extensively. Emile Durkheim wrote about societies such as the Australian aborigines without ever moving from his Paris *appartement*. Max Weber concerned himself with environments as remote as ancient India and China, and all his theories are carefully constructed from documentary records. Admittedly, the nineteenth-century intellectual environment was rather different from the present. The nineteenth century was a time of grand theory and generalization, of speculative as well as useful models. But during the twentieth century, as both social anthropologists and sociologists have narrowed their sights, concentrating on smaller, less ambitious empirical frameworks, the successful use of historical documents and perspectives has continued, stimulated especially by the facts of social change so obvious around us.

Examples of the use of historical materials and models are apparent in both the anthropological and sociological literature. Certainly Boas, one of the outstanding early figures in anthropology, did not lean toward history, but his followers, Kroeber, Lowie, Sapir, and others, though rigorously collecting facts by empirical methods, did look at problems in a historical dimension, utilizing, as much as possible, archeological and historical data. Their perspective, though not nearly as broad as that of the nineteenth-century evolutionary anthropologists, was still macrocosmic. The focuses were the dynamics and processes of large-scale cultural developments, cultural centers and climaxes, deriving important ideas from the European *Kulturkreise* school.

From the 1930s on there was a scaling down of the analytical dimension. Responsible for this were a number of important factors, primarily the increasing specialization in fieldwork and the influence of microcosmic functionalism, psychological and configurational approaches, and the booming new discipline of sociology itself. But despite the diminished concern with macroanalysis, anthropologists did not lose sight of the historical dimension. A major reason for this seems to have been that American anthropology has always been deeply influenced by the American Indian situation, which has been characterized by acculturation and rapid change (Murphy 1967). Most American anthropologists, until fairly recently, have received their training and won their theoretical spurs in the problems of Indian culture and society. Sturtevant (1966:9–10) has pointed out that a major stimulus to the use of documentary evidence in the study of North American Indian cultural change has been the Indian Claims Commission Act of 1946. Many anthropologists have been employed as witnesses by both the tribes concerned and the Department of Justice. As a result, very rich records, particularly in the National Archives, were discovered and utilized.

Largely within this American Indian tradition the discipline of ethnohistory developed. In the writings of ethnohistorians like Swanton, Fenton, Hickerson, Speck, Strong, Steward (1952), and Sturtevant (1966) there is detailed description and analysis of the changing social and cultural patterns of the Indian tribes, using both preanthropological and later professional records together with archeological and fieldwork evidence (see, for example, Laguna 1960). Archives and unpublished sources were used to considerable effect by Felix Keesing (1934, 1962), who worked not only in North America but also in Samoa, the Philippines, and New Zealand. In Europe too there was a continuing ethnological tradition from the nineteenth century utilizing historical materials, particularly in conjunction with archeological data (Penniman 1965). In addition to the American ethnohistorical focus, interest in social change in developing countries and in acculturation and modernization greatly stimulated historical perspectives in the so-called peasant literature (see, for example, Potter *et al.* 1967).

Much of the historical reconstruction, especially in the early ethnohistory, was cast in a wide framework embracing whole cultures and most facets of social organization, usually, though not always, from a perspective gained in the field. However, there are examples of the use of historical documents combined with fieldwork focusing on specific communities and particular theoretical problems. For instance, the Anderson's (1965) study of a village near Paris leans heavily on official records and the writings of a scholarly priest. Anthropologists have been most active in the study of political institutions, particularly from records of the colonial period (see, for example, I. M. Lewis 1968). There are many works considering historical aspects of economic activity (for example, Firth 1929) and religious behavior (for example, Evans-Pritchard 1949), and there is even a growing body of historical literature concerned with kinship—an area in which the historical record is in some respects the scantiest and least helpful.

There have been similar trends in American sociology (see, for example, Hofstadter and Lipset 1968:20ff). The re-emergence of historical and comparative sociology has gathered momentum throughout the 1960s, though there were important earlier movements (shown in works such as Sorokin 1962), and specific examples, such as Homans's (1960) study of thirteenth-century English villages or Smelser's (1959) analysis of changes in the Lancashire cotton industry. The recent revival has taken a number of forms—studies of past patterns of electoral behavior, changes in religious life, deviance (for example, K. T. Erikson 1966), national values, the intellectual climate, and so forth. As in the case of the anthropologists, however, an important stimulus was the developing world and the problems of "modernization."

Admittedly, not every cultural anthropologist or sociologist welcomed the historical perspective. The most extreme form of opposition was associated with the so-called structural–functionalist anthropologists, notably Malinowski and Radcliffe-Brown, and to some extent with the Parsonian functionalists.

Very generally, functionalist theories sought explanations in terms of contemporaneously interdependent variables. Theories of interdependence, with strong analogies to organismic theories in the physical sciences, implied or postulated a timelessness in which each element of the society constantly "functioned" to maintain the other parts and the whole in a kind of equilibrium. The "ethnographic present," or any other present, contained the essential elements of the past, present, and future.

For anthropologists, this orientation toward the present can be seen to be partly a result of methodological technique; a complete involvement for a relatively short period in remote and isolated localities. It was also the result of particular ideas about history and a strong reaction to the speculative use of sources by nineteenth-century writers. It was felt that local historical sources did not provide an accurate representation of past events. The representation of the past was part of the present, perhaps an explanation or a reflection of it. Events were not considered to be ordered in a proper time sequence, which was thought to be an impossibility without written records, but were embodied in oral traditions, myths, and legends, sources which related significantly to present events and structures. The "present orientation" of a people was also thought to be bolstered by a lack of a consciousness of their own history, or of the ordered passage of time and its events, or of the history of people and civilizations outside the village or tribal world (I. M. Lewis 1968: xiiff).

Despite this apparent antipathy to history, the functionalists were forced increasingly to involve themselves in historical problems. This was partly due to those, notably Evans-Pritchard, who pointed to the usefulness of history. But it was also the result of an increasing awareness of the obvious facts of social change in the tribal world, the resources that were available for studying these processes, and the previous "colonial" bias in any historical accounts (McCall 1964). Even Malinowski, when he left the sheltered waters of the Trobriands and came to Africa, concerned himself with the dynamics of cultural change (Malinowski 1945). Most of the anthropologists who went into the field after World War II were involved in situations of rapid change as empires crumbled. They were faced with a situation in which items of colonial culture had been imported or adopted. In consequence attention was shifted to the processes by which change had taken place and to the traditional state of society in which change was working. It came to be realised also that the social structure was neither static nor necessarily totally represented at any one time. To begin to comprehend the changes and to see the total social structure, it was necessary to look at historical data.

The notion of structure itself was consciously or unconsciously stretched in time and space and modified. Changes could take place over time without a fundamental change in society occurring—as, for example, in the cyclical models of Fortes (1958)—while all aspects of the social structure had a time component (their duration) without which they could not be understood (see Gluckman 1968). Gluckman also attempted to show that equilibrium was only attained through conflict and instability. A significant attack on the static equilibrium concepts came from Leach (1964) and others, who showed that alternative possibilities in the social structure could be present at different times and in different combinations.

Finally, alternative functionalist methods for understanding processes of change proved unwieldy or impossible. One alternative to historical analysis was synchronic comparison of present situations at different stages of change (for example, A. Cohen 1965). But it was very difficult, if not impossible, to assess the differential effects of differing environments and rates of change. Such a method also accentuated the problems of typicality and compounded any errors of choice. Another alternative was to make two or more diachronic field studies of the same society at different times (see, for example, Firth 1959). Apart from the practical and theoretical difficulties of replicating the original fieldwork, however, there still remained the problem of interpreting changes before or in between the field studies. As a result of all this, functionalists were forced to turn increasingly to historical aids in explanations (see, for example, Wilson 1939, J. A. Barnes 1967, M. G. Smith 1960, Braimah and Goody 1967, Southall 1961, Bailey 1960, Lloyd 1966, I. M. Lewis 1968).

Similarly, in the debates among American sociologists equilibrium theories were attacked by those [such as Coser (1964) and Dahrendorf (1959)] who considered change, conflict, and revolution to be at the heart of social inquiry, an emphasis that inevitably required historical analysis. Whereas the anthropological structural–functionalists stretched and modified their models to accommodate to change, the sociologists adapted differently. In Parson's writings, for instance, there is a coexistence of static and dynamic models, a combination some colleagues found "bewildering" (Gouldner 1956).

Links with History

In the developing interest in historical analysis contacts and links with historians were inevitably formed. There were admittedly some obstacles to communication. To a large extent, the disciplines were institutionally self-sufficient, with their own traditions, conventions, and loyalties (Aronson 1969). But there were also different theoretical emphases which have hindered cooperation to a greater or lesser extent. Many historians in the nineteenth century were most concerned to write narrative chronological compilations of fact, to show "how things really were" (*wie es eigentlich gewesen*), as Ranke put it. As a consequence, there was a great emphasis on studying situations as unique occurrences and events and as products of particular complex circumstances and contexts. The historical narrative was characteristically concerned with important political events, with nation-states and the great men who shaped national destinies rather than the norms of everyday communities. Events and situations were usually discussed in the context of a long period of time, usually well removed from the present. The quality of these narratives was judged by literary canons of style, and quantification was frowned on. Finally, documents usually provided the sole source material.

The historical profession, however, has been anything but monolithic, and there have always been nonconformist, "innovating" historians, as Hofstadter (Lipset and Hofstadter 1968:10) has called them. The reaction against the obsession for objective factual chronologies was strong (see Holloway in Burston and Thompson 1967 and Strout 1958) and was led in the United States by Becker and Beard. Some historians went as far as to see all history as subjective, though most would follow Collingwood's middle road (see Carr 1964:21): They would view interpretation as resting ultimately on an interaction between the facts as they probably happened and the historian's thoughts and the present situation. Although the emphasis on the specific has remained important, most historians now admit to a degree of generalization in every piece of historical analysis (Social Science Council 1954:128ff, Holloway in Burston and Thompson 1967). Formulation of hypotheses is common, though, in comparison with the social sciences, there is much less attempt to experiment, test, and verify by statistical or mathematical means or through disjunctive reasoning. Many historians in the computer age are involved in quantification which has—in economic history, for example—revolutionized techniques and theory. (Dollar and Jensen 1970.)

There has also been a long tradition of a broader social history not only as a backdrop to the political narrative but in its own right as well, initially in France (see, for example, Colloque 1967, and Bloch 1961 and 1966, and the works of Lefebvre, Granet, Dumezil, Braudel, de Coulanges, and so forth), and later in the United States (see, for example, Cochran 1964, Saveth 1964). Concepts and concentrations common in sociology and anthropology such as kinship, motivation, group structure, status, class, mobility, leadership, power, and roles, are increasingly used by historians.

Historians have also made microcosmic community studies in their own right (see, for example, Hoskins 1965 and Gras 1930) and there is growing use by American historians of the empirical material gathered by sociologists and anthropologists in studying topics such as urban communities and opinion samples (Handlin et al. 1966:31ff). Considerable use is being made of the highly empirical studies of the earlier researchers such as R. A. Woods and Kate Claghorn. Some historians (see Handlin et al. 1966:31ff) felt that later material such as the works of Park and the Chicago ecological school, or of Lloyd Warner and the Lynds, had to be used much more carefully. There were objections to what was felt to be a generalizing tendency and especially to anonymous localities and fictive persons. Unwarranted generalization was also felt to be characteristic of opinion samples. However, even the most conservative historian recognized that the sociological and anthropological literature contained information and insights of considerable value which could not be neglected.

Finally, historians have become increasingly concerned with contemporary history (see Barraclough 1964). Many historians have established their reputations working in recent periods (for example, Hofstadter, Shannon, May, Taylor, and Carr).

Most of the links between cultural anthropology, sociology, and history have been developed by innovators who share much common ground, though the importance of uniquity (that is, the small-scale study of a particular society or situation) and the primacy of facts in cultural anthropology (see, for example, Mead 1951) have been conducive to the formation of some contacts with the more traditional historians. Cooperation has taken the form of symposia [for example, the Social Science Research Council (Hofstadter and Lipset 1968, Lipset and Hofstadter 1968)], specific projects, (such as the Norristown project at the University of Pennsylvania), institutions concerned with common problems (for example, the Research Center in Entrepreneurial History at Harvard, and the Research Center in Economic Development and Cultural Change in Chicago), and area and regional studies.

Contributing to the rapprochement between the disciplines has been the growing awareness by social scientists that a first priority in any historical analysis is the professional handling of the basic data source—that is, documents. In this field the historians, both the conservatives and the innovators, have developed over the years rigorous methods for utilizing documentary material. In the next chapter these methods, so important in historical analysis, will be examined in detail, indicating the ways in which they have been, or can be, integrated with more traditional sociological and cultural anthropological approaches.

Further Reading

The different approaches of historians and anthropologists and sociologists have been widely discussed in the literature. The institutional differences between cultural anthropology and history are discussed by Cohn (1962), who pretends that he is doing fieldwork among the historians. Kroeber (1935) (see also Kroeber 1963) provides an early discussion, while Evans-Pritchard (1961) makes an eloquent plea for more history in social anthropology, especially the history of French social historians like Marc Bloch. This topic is further debated in the structural–functionalist context by Schapera (1962), M. G. Smith (1962), and I. M. Lewis (1968). The last work has helpful bibliographies. Useful material on the history of anthropological theory is provided by Harris (1968), while functionalism is discussed critically by P. S. Cohen (1968) and Goldschmidt (1966).

Ethnohistorical connections are lucidly discussed by Sturtevant (1966), and further material is supplied by Fenton (1952). Keesing (1953) offers a bibliography of culture-change literature up to 1950, and later trend reports appear in the *Stanford Biennial Review of Anthropology* (Siegel *et al.* 1959 *et seq.*, especially Murphy 1967). Spicer (1961) has edited a useful anthology. Interesting material is provided by Steward (1955), while Mead (1951) outlines the parallels between anthropology and "traditional" history. Students should also look at the journal *Ethnohistory*.

The Social Science Research Council reports on history and the social sciences are a mine of information and comment. The first report, with contributions by Gottschalk, Kluckhohn, and Angell (1945), deals with the use of personal documents; the second (Social Science Research Council 1954) presents an ambitious statement on the links, real and potential, between the disciplines; the third (Gottschalk 1963) considers, more cautiously, the use of generalization in history. A new series, the Sociology of American History (Lipset and Hofstadter 1968, Hofstadter and Lipset 1968), contains essays which clearly demonstrate the links, discussing, specifically, quantitative methods, census returns, social characteristics of investors in nineteenth-century Boston, millionaires, corruption, religion, the frontier thesis and the class structure. Quantitative methods are discussed more fully by Dollar and Jensen (1970).

Further useful information on the links between the disciplines are contained in works written or edited by Ware (1940), Thrupp (1957), Halpern (1957), Saveth (1964), Cochran (1964), Dovring (1960), Eisenstadt (1966), Cahnman and Boskoff (1964), and Krug (1967). Aronson (1969) summarizes some of the obstacles to a rapprochement, and Thomas (1963) and Hughes (1964) represent the historian's point of view. Handlin and his associates (1966) provide a comprehensive review of all aspects of American historical research. The student should also consult periodicals in which historians and sociologists cooperate, such as *Comparative Studies in Society and History, Explorations in Entrepreneurial History*, and *Economic Development and Cultural Change*.

There are many guides to the uses of historical data written by historians.

Bloch's (1954) book is still very useful. Other recent volumes worth looking at include those by Elton (1967), Thomson (1969), Carr (1964), Gottschalk (1969), Kitson Clark (1967), and Nevins (1962). Barraclough (1964) is specifically concerned with contemporary history, while Leff (1969) and Meyerhoff (1959) deal especially with philosophical problems. A selection of writings on American history with a special section on relations with other disciplines has been edited by Eisenstadt (1966). Other interesting disucssions of recent trends are included in the special history issues of *Encounter* (1969), the *Journal of Contemporary History* (1968), *Daedalus* (1968), and the London *Times Literary Supplement* (1966). Informative essays on the work of American and European historians can be found in books edited by Wish (1960) and Halperin (1960). Interesting comments are made and a good bibliography on schools of thought is provided by Barzun and Graff (1957). Two basic and long-used manuals are those by Handlin and his associates (1966) and Hockett (1955).

There are many specific examples of the use of historical perspectives in anthropological or sociological problems in addition to those mentioned in the text. Spicer (1962) presents a detailed ethnohistory of the Indians of the Southwest informed by the author's own field experience in the region. Ewers' (1955) *The Horse in Blackfoot Indian Culture* combines a variety of different sources in analysis. Other good examples of ethnohistorical methods can be found in the works of Keesing (1962), Trigger (1969), and Hickerson (1962, 1970) while Balandier (1968) provides an interesting reconstruction of life in the Congo 300 years ago. Peter Laslett (1965) provides a brilliant survey of society in Stuart England, while George Homans (1960) explores the thirteenth-century context. W. I. Thomas and F. Znaniecki's (1958) study of the Polish peasant in Europe and America is still a classic, while J. Zubrzycki (1964) explores migrant problems in Australia. Tilly (1964) has written an illuminating study of the Vendée region in France in the revolutionary period.

Much historical discussion in the social anthropological literature has been concerned with political changes. Papers on political developments in several African societies and also in ancient Rome, Albania, and the Scottish Highlands are included in I. M. Lewis's (1968) anthology. Other important studies are those by Cohn and Singer (1968) and Bailey (1960) (India); Leach (1964) (Burma); Cunnison (1959), J. A. Barnes (1967), Gullick (1958), Jones (1963), and M. G. Smith (1960) (Africa).

In the economic field Firth (1929) pioneered with a study of the economic organization of the New Zealand Maori. More recently, Pitt (1970) has attempted to use historical and fieldwork materials in discussing economic development in Samoa. Other economic studies utilizing historical perspectives and documents are Smelser's (1959) analysis of the Lancashire cotton industry, Carrasco's (1959) study of land tenure in Tibet, Beidelman's (1959) account of the *jajmani* system, Geertz's (1963) on social change in Java, or in the studies of classic societies by Polanyi and his associates (1957).

In the field of religion two important studies are Evans-Pritchard's (1949) analysis of the development of the Islamic Sanusi sect in Cyrenaica and Kai Erikson's recent (1966) discussion of a Puritan community in seventeenth-century

New England. Also of interest are Middleton's (1960) study of the religious authority of the Lugbara, I. M. Lewis's (1966) account of spirit possession cults, and Worsley's (1957) study of cargo cults. Some recent studies of myth (for example, Levi-Strauss 1970) have leaned heavily on documents collected by missionaries and others.

Time depth or documentary evidence has been used to advantage in studying changing kinship terminologies [for example, by Anderson (1963) and M. G. Smith (1962)], genealogies [by Cunnison (1959), Bohanan (1952), and Peters (1960)], the changing functions of lineages [by A. Cohen (1965)], and the effects of socioeconomic change on kinship systems [by Gough (1952)]. Other useful studies of kinship systems using historical sources are those by Eggan (1966) (American Indian), Nakane (1967) (Japan), Lounsbury (1964) (ancient Rome), and Lancaster (1958) (Anglo-Saxon). There are important comments on historical aspects of demography in *Daedalus* (n.2 1968). A useful study concentrating on the history of actual communal units is Mosely's account of the *zadruga* (in Ware 1940).

Finally, two books just to hand, should be read by those particularly interested in the functionalist debate in sociology. These are R. W. Friedrichs, *Sociology of Sociology* (1970, New York: Free Press) and A. Gouldner, *The Coming Crisis of Western Sociology* (1970, New York: Basic).

2

Major Sources of
Documentary Material

What Is a Document?

THE FIRST PROBLEM is to define (if somewhat arbitrarily) what we mean by the term "documentary evidence." Generally, we mean information which has been written about a subject, as opposed to oral testimony, archeological artifacts, or pictorial evidence, and so forth, though some historians [for example, Gottschalk (1969:57)] prefer to call all recorded evidence by the generic term "documentation." Documents may be written by hand (manuscript) or reproduced mechanically (typescript, mimeograph, printed materials, or the like), produced in limited quantities or widely published.

Documents may be further classified according to the proximity of the person recording the facts. Eyewitness or firsthand accounts are usually called primary documents or sources, and all other accounts are secondary sources. Other kinds of classification involve degree of originality or observer subjectivity (Gottschalk 1969:58). Large accumulations of manuscripts or other documents when institutionally organized are called archives, while smaller accumulations are often called collections.

Locating the Material—General Points

The first job in historical research is to locate material relevant to the subject being studied. We are presuming here that the research worker already has a subject in mind, for one type of historical method is to explore documentary sources with a view to establishing a worthwhile subject for research.

The first call is always to the library, where catalogs, bibliographies, guides to archival and manuscript sources, and other research aids give a general indication of the available material. Follow-up letters to the relevant institutions may be necessary to acquire more detailed knowledge, as manuscript and unpublished sources particularly are not always described in the catalogs or bibliographies. This is particularly true for anthropologists working in African or Asian contexts. In this case the preferred method is simply to locate the central offices of those institutions that have figured in the history of the area in which the anthropologist is interested. At this stage of research it is useful to draw up a list of sources and a timetable for consultation, especially if sources are scattered over a wide area.

In the following sections some of the major categories of sources which are likely to be of use are described.

Public and Official Archives

Public archives, consisting of documents collected and preserved by governments or official bodies, are always important sources. In particular, since many anthropologists are concerned with Afro-Asian societies, often the first task is to examine the colonial archives. The most important, and certainly the largest, collections of colonial records are contained in the national archives of the mother countries. In England, for example, the Public Record Office contains the records of government departments. Some departmental papers are only deposited after seventy or eighty years, but those most likely to interest the anthropologist, the Colonial Office and Commonwealth Relations Office papers, are about fifteen years in arrears, while the Foreign Office papers run about thirty years behind. Many of the papers, for example, the gazettes, minutes, journals, official papers, and statistics of the territories, are open to consultation, though the office papers (correspondence, reports, and such) are currently closed for thirty years, unless permission (only given in exceptional circumstances) is obtained from the Secretary of State. In addition to the Public Record Office papers there are also important collections retained in the government departments themselves, for example, in the former India Office.

Similar kinds of records are available about peoples who were not, or have ceased to be, part of the larger colonial empires. In the United States, Canada, South Africa, Australia, and New Zealand there are, or have been, specific government departments concerned with the administration of non-European peoples, the papers of which eventually find their way into the respective national archives. For example, in the United States there are a vast number of documents on the American Indian, especially in the Department of the Interior files, most of which has not been touched by anthropologists.

In these large public archives what kinds of records are likely to be of interest? To a large extent this depends on the research focus, but whatever this is, always of considerable relevance are the broad outlines of contact with Europeans, and the consequent demographic, economic, and political changes.

The first records likely to be of use are the papers of the explorers and travelers, many of whose voyages were officially sponsored. Often the explorers' accounts are published and therefore easier to reach through the library, but there are still many unpublished accounts, and those published do not always contain the original texts in full. For example, the famous journals of Captain Cook's voyages to the South Pacific in the eighteenth century were only recently published (Beaglehole 1955) in the original form. When Cook returned to England, it was felt that the account of a rough sea captain would not do adequate justice to such an important event and the job was given to a writer who never went on the voyage and whose prose, while perhaps admired by the literary critics of the time, is neither particularly accurate nor as evocative as the careful observations of Cook himself.

Later I will go into the question of accuracy more fully. It is important at the planning stage of research, however, to be aware of the approximate reliability of various kinds of documents. With some notable exceptions, the early explorers are not generally as accurate or as relevant as later observers such as the missionaries. In many cases the explorers had only fleeting contacts with the peoples they described. Consequently, one finds ludicrous statements such as the claim that the men of the Nicobar Islands had tails (the way in which they wore their loin cloths) or the observation that the Samoans wore brocaded trousers (actually a tattooed pattern).

The same comment applies even when there is some kind of elementary quantification. Again in the South Pacific, there are some wild estimates of early population figures, based on such vague indicators as a count of wisps of smoke as the explorer drifted along the coast. The major exceptions are those cases where there was longer residence, for example, in the careful writings of the scientists who often accompanied the voyages, and in descriptions of climactic events (wars, revolutions) witnessed firsthand.

The files of the diplomatic representatives are a second important documentary source, especially in the precolonial period or in noncolonial areas. An important function of the consuls or ambassadors was to provide information on the areas to which they were accredited. In addition to political facts, this information always included a considerable amount of commercial data since the consular responsibility was as much to stimulate trade as to protect property and persons. In many areas of Afro-Asia there was a very thin line between official and commercial activities. In regular diplomatic reports there is often information on social or economic change, especially cash crop production and land usage, wage labor, demography, trading, and communications, and so forth.

The colonial period itself contains the first really important mass of relevant documentation. Colonial government papers consist of several important divisions. First, there are papers dealing with general policy. These papers are usually located in the metropolitan country and refer in a definite sense to the social and political structure of this country. Second, there are the papers concerned with the implementation of policy in the colonial area. Within this group there is usually an important division of papers which refer to "native affairs," often emanating from a specific government department in the colony. Again within this group of papers there are the reports that are sent home, the files in the colony itself, and the local files on which the reports are based. The latter two, since they contain detailed local information, are of great interest. Not all relevant government information is gathered in one place, however. The separation of "native" from other affairs disappeared in many colonial areas, especially as new departments emerged to take over specific governmental functions. The implementation of policy was carried out through a complex legal apparatus, and the papers concerning the formulation of laws and their implementation can also be an important source.

What kinds of records are likely to be useful in these papers? In some areas ethnographical studies themselves were commissioned, or notes on customs collected, either by colonial officers themselves or much less often by local people. An example of the usefulness of local records of this kind are a chief's descriptions of the emirate of Abuja in northern Nigeria. M. G. Smith (1960) has used this document to considerable effect in analyzing political changes in this area.

Often such information was the by-product of special political or economic studies. For instance, there is much information in the papers of the Spanish colonial *visita* (see, for example, Murra 1967) used in the Spanish colonies to gather information on local peoples, to help assess tribute and taxes due, and generally to provide a solid base for colonial administration.

Within the colonial records there are important statistical records as well, particularly the censuses, but also taxation returns, production figures, and the like. These macrocosmic figures have special kinds of value. Even in a small developing country, the fieldworker can only cover a fraction of the population in time and space. More significant still, official figures collected under fiat may not be revealed to the private researcher. Such information is a supplement or a cross-check, even when the fieldworker is present.

The departments of the colonial government also contain valuable information. Judicial records contain data on questions such as land tenure, titles, exchange, marriage, divorce, inheritance, and criminal offenses. Education and medical matters are extensively covered. School registers, hospital records, as well as correspondence, reports, and the like, can be useful. Political institutions are well treated, especially when there are political troubles (with commissions or detailed reports on them), or during the period in which colonial powers were constitution making or preparing for independence. Other important political items are to be found in the poll returns for local or national elections, minutes of meetings of government bodies, especially if they are available at local levels. In many archives there are biographical files on important local personalities.

Less often there are special documentary collections which can be of critical importance to the anthropologist. An example are the papers of the *Commissie van Onderzoek naar de Mindere Welvaart der Inlandsche* (Commission for the Investigation of the Diminishing Welfare of the Indonesian Population in Indonesia). This commission, inaugurated by the Dutch colonial authorities in 1902, involved 594 research workers who for twelve years took a huge questionnaire, designed to provide information on all aspects of rural life, around to Javanese villages. Thirty large volumes resulted from the investigations, and although some unreliability and superficiality exist, any researcher in this area cannot ignore such a mountain of empirical material.

As far as the anthropologist is concerned, there are, admittedly, gaps and deficiencies in these official records, and once again these limits have to be realized at an early stage of research. Possibly the greatest drawback is that colonial officials were often expatriates, on short-term service, living apart from local society, often ignorant of the local language and customs. It has been said that the colonial officers' view of local society consisted of what their houseboys (or housegirls) could tell them. Unfair though this comment may be (and there were certainly important exceptions), many officers held stereotypes of local society which were reflected in official reporting. "Native" social structure was regarded in terms of either excessively idealistic or derogatory models (the noble savage or the backward primitive), though these models may still be of value to the anthropologist, especially if his interest is in stereotypes and race relations. Another drawback is that information and statistics, especially in the home country records, may be generalized for the whole territory without referring to sources of information or local variations. This is a reflection of the highly centralized political structure in many colonial areas. More important, perhaps, again in the home country records, is the official line often taken in reports and memorandums. There may also be very minimal reporting of highly confidential matters. A further constraint, especially in very recent times, is the extensive use of the telephone for communication, leaving, of course, no (or very sparse) records.

Some of these defects may be rectified in the exploration of archives in the colonial area itself, where the record is franker and much fuller. In addition, for the anthropologist interested in microcosmic studies of particular localities, local official records have a special value. The snag here is that local archives, if they have been officially established, may not be well organized, and relevant records may have been destroyed or lost. Paper-eating bugs and rats flourish in tropical archives, and documents are not usually considered sacrosanct. These problems tend to increase as one descends the political scale, and there will probably be few government records at the village level. Even if there are records, they are likely to be thrown together in an old shed or cupboard. The anthropologist can himself help, especially if he has rapport with government officials, by asking that documents may be preserved. The officials may well be glad to have a place to put unwanted paper.

Finally, there is the great problem of restricted access either to confidential papers or to recent materials. Most European archives insist on at least a 20- to 30-year rule. In the case of the personal dossiers in the Ministry of Foreign Affairs in Paris there is a 150-year limit, and some archives are rumored to exclude researchers for 300 years. Consultation difficulties are eased if the researcher has some kind of quasi-official status, as some anthropologists have had when working in their own countries' colonial archives. In the case of census records, especially the valuable manuscript returns, there are often extensive restrictions, for example, 72 years in the United States. Only in exceptional cases can these restrictions be waived. Another problem may be the policy destruction of important documents, for example, voting papers in some countries. However, very often local rules may not be so stringent, and gaps can be partially filled.

Although most official colonial papers are to be found in the public archives or in government departments, an alternative source, especially for material which has been duplicated, is in the larger libraries of the home countries. For example, in Great Britain the British Museum, the Bodleian Library at Oxford, and the University Library at Cambridge have huge depositories of colonial and common-wealth material, and there are important collections in the Bibliotheque Nationale in Paris, the Library of Congress, and so forth. Use of these sources may save the research worker much time since the public archives are often very crowded. In some cases too, there is official material in such places which cannot be found elsewhere. For example, Oxford, the home of lost causes, is also a center for unwanted colonial and commonwealth documents that might otherwise have been destroyed or lost. This valuable collection includes diaries, memoirs, and letters of former colonial civil servants.

Noncolonial archives in Europe and America present only slightly different problems, though the scale of available coverage and time depth is much vaster. Consequently, there is a greater premium on efficient organization of research. Problems of access and availability tend also to be greater, and it is not often that the research worker has the advantage of being part of the establishment, or having favored status. In addition, there are always important collections in the departments or at subnational levels.

These kinds of official archive have been used, from the nineteenth cen-tury, by sociologists interested in a wide variety of theoretical problems, including such classics as Emile Durkheim's study of suicide (Durkheim 1951). Topics investigated through birth, death, and marriage statistics include factors affecting fertility levels, premarital sex habits, preference for male offspring, religious identification, and occupational status, divorce, the incidence of genius, mobility, and so on (Webb et al. 1966:51–65).

Political records, votes, roll calls, ballots, speeches, electoral rolls, and the like have been extensively used by political sociologists (Webb et al. 1966:65), while judicial records, social workers' papers, and so forth, are particularly valu-able in the study of deviance and social problems. An important early work in this field was W. I. Thomas and F. Znaniecki's (1958) use of court records and other sources to portray the difficulties encountered by Polish people on arrival in Amer-ica. Another example of the skilful use of court records is Kai Erikson's recent (1966) analysis of deviance in seventeenth-century New England using the witch-craft trials material. The list of official sources that have been used by sociologists or anthropologists is, in fact, very long, including tax files, records of land deal-ings, power, water pressure, and parking meter returns (Webb et al. 1966:73).

An important category within these official archives is that based on individual local or small-scale returns, which can be integrated with microcosmic analysis. Of this type of record the census is one of the most important.

Census materials contain detailed local information, especially demographic and kinship information. In Europe, North America, and countries such as Japan these records have a considerable time depth stretching well back into the eight-eenth century and sometimes beyond. For example, in Japan censuses in embryonic form date from 1644 and were established on a national basis in 1721. These latter censuses, designed to aid tax collection (Ninbetsu-aratame) or sup-press Christianity (Shumon-aratane), provide not only the usual demographic data but also data regarding such topics as occupation, status, land tenure and use, house size and ownership, capital, villages from which wives and servants came, and length of employment of servants. Each year an official added to the record retirements of heads of households, birth, deaths, and marriages, details of succession and inheritance, changes of address, and details of immigrants and emigrants (Nakane 1967:47–49).

For the cultural anthropologist the study of local official documents is easily integrated with the field work program. Every fieldworker knows periods of relative idleness when little appears to be happening in the village and nobody wants to be interviewed. These periods can profitably be used for the study of local files. In addition, it may actually improve the fieldworker's status and legitimacy in official eyes. The mystique of participant observation is not fully appreciated by many officials, but an interest in the files, to which many officials have attitudes of great respect and importance, is readily understood. Contact with documents and files, so much a part of official ritual and behavior, may well impart to the fieldworker a certain official status. The anthropologist is no longer a somewhat arty outsider asking curious questions but, like the many itinerant observers, experts, and visitors from the higher echelons of government, a serious individual concerned with the questions of local social, economic, and political development. As we shall see later, however, a very great interest in the documents may increase the suspicion against the fieldworker and possibly act to his disadvantage in other fieldwork activities.

Local records also have the advantage that they gather in one place a large amount of local and specific information, eliminating the time-consuming task that occurs in the larger archives of searching for a reference to a village or some person. However, the local records are never complete and are supplements not replacements for the larger records, even when government is decentralized.

For example, in Switzerland, the smallest political authority, the commune, comprising usually a village and its environs, has a great deal of independence. It levies important taxes and formulates a considerable number of by-laws. In addition, however, the higher authorities (the district, the canton, the federal government) are deeply involved in village activities, and there are representatives of these agencies in the villages. The documentary situation reflects this division of authority. Village files contain a good deal of information on village history, particularly on political relations with the outside world. But there is very little, for example, on demography or economic conditions, documentation which has flowed out of the village into a wide range of dispersed sources.

Other more technical problems are likely to occur. Local resources usually do not stretch to competently staffing the archives. There are not people to properly file the material or to supervise its use. Apart from the technical problems of access, there may be great uncertainty about assessing the confidentiality of files. However good the anthropologist's rapport is with the village authorities, some important files may be arbitrarily withheld simply because there is nobody to decide, or no rule, about academic consultation.

Government papers at the national or local level form the bulk of relevant official papers, but there may be, in addition, other relevant official papers. In this category are the papers or publications of official or quasi-official organizations (research institutes, and the like) and the "international" papers (from such bodies as the League of Nations and the United Nations). In general these papers are of lesser interest than the detailed files. Like George Eliot's humanitarianism, perception and understanding of the local scene and society seem to vary inversely with distance. Many of these reports and publications, notably those from the international bodies, are based on a most cursory acquaintance with local society. They really emanate from the studies and offices of Geneva or New York, and, consequently, they reflect the values and rules of these organizations. Often too, they deal with future and ideal situations rather than present actualities. The commitment to print and the constraints of political sensitivity generally reduces value still further. With some exceptions, reporting tends to be very generalized, highly formalized, and uninformative from the anthropological or sociological point of view.

Mission and Church Sources

The second extremely important collection of documentary material, particularly for the anthropologist, is the archives of the religious institutions, especially the missionary societies. The missionaries were sometimes the first to visit non-European peoples and often the first to make detailed studies. Like the administrations, internal pressures, and philosophies influence the broad form which the mission record takes. But significantly, missionaries often regarded the detailed and accurate recording of local language and customs as an essential part of the job of communicating the gospel or a worthwhile activity *sui generis.*

Mission archives are usually maintained in the first instance by the mother societies, most of which are located in Europe or America. Important sources in these archives are the regular letters which the missionaries wrote home, and in the journals which they kept. Often the mother societies have also inherited the papers of the missionaries, containing valuable diaries, notes on customs, non-official letters, and linguistic notes which the missionary retained. As in the case of administrative records, there are also mission sources in the fieldwork area which contain much more local detail, and in all probability, valuable unexpurgated data which are not included in the reports sent home.

Ethnographic information in the mission record will probably touch on things of central importance to the anthropologist. Many missionaries had a good grasp of the language derived from long residence, and from a study of grammar, usage, and vocabulary. Many were also anxious to record the details of traditional customs and oral literature, partly from a humanistic or scholarly interest but also as an aid in the process of conversion. Since these notes are often based on information or observation from very early stages of contact, they can be of great value. Some of the best works of this genre have been published: for example, *The Jesuit Relations* in the Americas; and the works of William

Ellis, W. W. Gill, George Turner, C. Strehlow, and R. Codrington in the Pacific; Bishop Callaway, David Livingstone, H. A. Junod, John Roscoe, and Edward Smith in Africa; and E. R. Huc, Abbé Dubois, and Hans Scharer in Asia (see References). However, these represent at best only summaries of information gathered, and they often present material which had to pass censorship before publication. So it will probably be necessary to go to the unpublished archives. An increasing number of missionaries have also received anthropological training, and their notes may be of a high standard. The work of Father W. Schmidt (1926–1955) and his students is a good example.

The mission record often has to be used with caution, however, not usually, as in the official files, because of superficiality but rather because the missionaries were deeply involved in the process of conversion, an involvement which inevitably has colored reporting. This difficult problem of bias and interpretation will be discussed in Chapter 4. A second problem involves restrictions on the use of missionary archives. In some archives there are very stringent restrictions on access, closing up documents for as many as 300 years to the nonfaithful.

The church records themselves are another very important type of religious archive. Some of the most ancient and continuous historical records in Europe are in parish archives. Very early and extensive records of contact are also preserved in many Afro-Asian diocesan headquarters, presbyteries, schools, and private homes. The local churches in Afro-Asia were important vehicles for promoting literacy. In East Africa, for example, early Christians were known as "readers." In a situation where reading and writing were regarded as in some way miraculous, and the arrival of a letter was a happening, papers were carefully preserved. First and foremost, these records related to religious and ecclesiastical matters. In particular, accounts of disciplinary issues affecting both clergy and laity are valuable sources for demonstrating the impact of Christian morality on existing beliefs and customs. In addition, church records contain very important kinship data—for example, birth, death, confirmation, and marriage registrations. There are also important economic details in records about school fees, church dues, building projects, church expenses, and so forth. Finally, there are important data in the minutes of parish meetings, parish circulars, and the like.

Business and Company Sources

A third important element in the historical record are company and business sources. In many parts of the colonial world economic activities were conducted by official or semiofficial trading companies, and their papers have been deposited in public archives or relevant government departments. Most company records, however, are to be found at the companies themselves. In addition, a certain amount of information about companies (articles of association, lists of directors, shareholders, details of capital formation, and so forth) may be found at official registeries.

Company papers contain most valuable information on economic activities.

Comprehensive account books can provide the key to patterns of production, consumption, exchange, credit, and debt, for traders in many parts of Afro-Asia monopolized buying, selling, and lending functions in the villages. Pay sheets for firms employing village labor can provide significant data on patterns of wage labor and the prices of services. Personnel records, staff books, union records, and such provide much sociological information, especially during times of con flict (for example, strikes), when the dominant influences in the social structure are brought into high relief (cf. Whyte 1969). Extremely valuable too are the papers of local companies, especially those run by local people. These papers provide details on the growth of entrepreneurial activities. In addition to company accounts there may also be journals or ships' logs (kept by every ship) which throw light especially on the early stages of contact, as well as describing local society, particularly around the port areas. Fine collections of this kind of material can be found in the Hudson Bay Company records in London, in the United States National Archives, at the Peabody Museum in Salem (traders), or in museums in New Bedford and Providence (whalers). A special category of company record is bank or insurance files, with their information on savings, capital formation, and credit.

Last, but by no means least, is the sociological information thrown up in the market research surveys which have become an essential part of modern business. Modern management recognizes that social and psychological facts play an important part in determining consumer preferences. Since data is often gathered through ill-conceived questionnaires or inadequate samples, however, it may be of dubious value. One ridiculous example was a beer company which sought to explain the low consumption of their beer in an African country by pointing to a (supposedly) traditional ritual during which the peoples' front teeth were pulled out, making it (supposedly) impossible for them to pronounce the beer's name. Yet market surveys may yield information (for example, consumer expenditure) which is difficult to obtain elsewhere, and there are a number of important studies derived from these sources (for example, Abrams 1968). In addition, a number of companies undertake general surveys of social structure as a background for their market studies.

There are many difficulties in the use of company records. In Afro-Asia the companies, like the administrations, are often remote from the village scene. However, there have been cases of traders who lived in a village, often taking a much greater part in local society than the missionaries or administrators. For example, in Samoa during the German colonial period, in order to help trade, the semiofficial trading company insisted that its employees speak the local language, marry locally, and be able to get on with people without quarreling. Unfortunately, the village traders rarely committed themselves to writing, and often their account books consist only of dog-eared pieces of paper.

Another big difficulty is the consultation of company records. Many companies simply do not allow access, and those that do generally have very stringent rules for use, including a long closed period. Most difficult of all to reach is the market research material since this often has considerable commercial value.

Scholarly Institutions

Another important source for both official and nonofficial papers is the scholarly institutions: universities, museums, libraries, research institutions, and learned societies. One good example of the value of this kind of source is the important collection of American Indian manuscripts or copies in the American Philosophical Society archives. A number of large universities have also acquired valuable collections on specific areas or interests. For example, many of the manuscripts of the American Board of Commissioners for Foreign Missions are deposited at Harvard. In addition, these institutions contain the unpublished notes, theses, and papers of scholars and researchers who are interested in the fieldwork area. In many parts of Afro-Asia there is now a considerable mass of material collected by professional social scientists. A heavy concentration of this kind of material is likely to be found in the university, research institute, or museum in the fieldwork area, and such material is usually of great relevance and interest. Affiliation to one of these local institutions not only allows the researcher to utilize results of other experts' knowledge but also may well give him the necessary status and introductions for the use of official sources.

Local learned or other socieites, especially those with ethnographic, folkloric, or sociological interests, often have relevant data and knowledge about data location or methods of utilization. From some of the larger associations of this kind (for example, the American Folklore Society and the American Association for State and Local History) it is possible to obtain information on the best methods of collecting and examining localized and specialized documents (see, for example, Goldstein 1964 and Parker 1944), and there are even new insights on such familiar topics to anthropologists as genealogies (see, for example, Doane 1960). Other national local history societies may maintain extensive archives, like the Japan Association for the Study of Local History (*Chiho-Kenkyo-Kyo-gikai*) or send out detailed ethnographic questionnaires to villages. Local ethnographic or sociological sources can be very valuable, even in countries where there is strict censorship, as the Dunns (E. Dunn and S. Dunn 1967) have shown in their study of the peasants of central Russia.

Finally, of course, libraries contain vast collections of secondary source material (that is, documentation by persons who were not eyewitnesses) which may provide analytical clues or leads to further primary source material.

Letters, Diaries, and Private Papers

So far we have considered the archives of institutions, but in addition, there are vast collections of what are sometimes called "private papers." Very important in this category are papers written by people involved in the political, religious, or economic institutions outside the course of duty. These records may have the advantage that the writer does not feel constrained by his official duties or obligations. Another important group of private papers are letters—those written by people both great (see, for example, Sussman 1963) and humble. Such letters were used to considerable effect in W. I. Thomas and F. Znaniecki's (1958) classic study of the Polish peasant in Europe and America. Diaries too may reveal important sociological information, as Janowitz (Janowitz and Daugherty 1958: 732–735) has shown in his study of German soldiers. Letters can also be used to bring up to date or fill out the fieldwork record when the research worker is not in the field. Information can be provided by trusted informants when the fieldwork is finished and the researcher finds himself many miles outside the fieldwork area, with embarrassing gaps in his field notes.

There are, however, important restrictions in the use of letters, diaries, and kindred material. Tracing these records can be a problem. The private papers of important persons may be preserved in public archives. For example, the British Museum possesses 50,000 manuscripts of this kind relating to India, Pakistan, Ceylon, and Burma alone. The United States Library of Congress also has a huge collection of "private" manuscript materials or microfilm. Some kinds of letters (for example, those submitted to newspapers) are published and therefore easy to locate.

A far greater problem is to locate the private papers of lesser known people. Most are still held by the families, though there are institutions in many countries (for example, the Historical Manuscripts Commission in England) which have extensive lists and can help in the search.

Then there is the difficulty of securing permission for use. Many people in many cultures are unwilling to make personal documents available, even if they contain only the most mundane material (Riley 1963:242–243). Again, there are only a limited number of social situations in which the participants are separate and there is a flow of letters. Different cultures also place different emphases on the importance of letter writing or diary keeping and the form of content of these sources. The degree of literacy is relevant also to the kind of document produced and its interpretation. Webb and his colleagues (1966:105) ask whether those letters written for the Polish peasants by scribes (W. I. Thomas and F. Znaniecki: 1958) present a different picture than those written by the people themselves. Finally, in a culture such as that in the United States where there is mass circulation of letters by organizations for political, advertising, or other purposes, there are special problems of preservation and interpretation. Such "junk," as Dexter calls this kind of material in his study of letters to congressmen (Dexter and White 1964:394ff), may have to be quickly consigned to the wastepaper basket.

Another interesting source to be found in private houses are photograph albums and ancillary documentation such as postcards, souvenirs, and mementos, family obituaries, and miscellaneous clippings. Those sources are important in themselves, indicating family movement, kinship patterns, friendship, and other associational interests. As important, photograph albums especially are something families in many cultures are happy to show, and they may prompt people to talk about relatives or places, subjects which would not usually come up in conversations and reference to which may normally be considered as impolite.

When dealing with private papers, the research worker may have the chance to preserve or create his own collection of documentation. This may be a costly business, but there are often people who will welcome the chance of writing about local customs, life histories, details of daily activities, attitudes, and such, as well as myths and legends, and may even have a script ready. If not voluntarily provided, instant documentation can be obtained if a cooperative schoolteacher, for example, will allow senior pupils to write an essay on a chosen subject. Certainly, there are many families who preserve, or are willing to preserve, letters that are written to family members.

Literature

By literature we mean works written by people who are generally not professional social scientists and who present a subjective or fictitious picture. The first important category for our purposes is the travel literature. Soon after the period of the explorers, private travelers were wandering around and writing about Europe and beyond. In 1785 Gibbon noted that there were 40,000 English people living on the continent, and this was before the tradition of the grand tour. Geographical literature began to appear in England by the end of the sixteenth century, including ethnologically important works like Prat's (1554) description of the "country of Aphrique" (Bennett 1952:122). In France between 1600 and 1660, 400 books were published relating to voyages outside Europe. Certainly, in many cases the records of these voyages were inconsequential, superficial tourist diaries, but in some cases, especially by the eighteenth and nineteenth centuries, there were detailed descriptions of particular localities and aspects of the social structure. For example, there are penetrating descriptions of social institutions in the works of Stendhal (Beyle 1962) Rousseau, Voltaire, Balzac, Baudelaire, Mrs. Craddock, Boswell, Gibbon, Dumas *Père*, Stevenson (1892), Edward Lear, de Tocqueville, Siegfried, and so forth (see References). There is even sometimes precise empirical documentation. Two good examples are Arthur Young's detailed description of the socioeconomy of the *ancien régime* in rural France (Young 1929) or Robert Louis Stevenson's record of political struggles in Samoa in his *Footnote to History* (Stevenson 1892).

One of the drawbacks of much travel description is that it is overwhelmingly the product of outsiders' observations and interpretations. Accounts by local travelers do exist, but particularly in Afro-Asia, they are rarely printed and have to be gleaned from private papers and collections. One of the few exceptions has been a recent collection of narratives by African travelers in the slave-trade era (Curtin 1967).

Although the descriptive accounts are the most valuable, the material contained in fictional form should not be entirely ignored. First, it may provide valuable clues or leads to significant factors in the social structure. Often it is from direct observation of societal facts, from ethnographic realism, as Oscar Lewis calls it (1959:18), that the literary realism of the novel or short story is derived. The novelists have a great interest in the minutiae of social life, in psychological factors, in watching closely the daily life of a family or a person rather than a community, in things, in short, which are seldom recorded in any other place.

In the so-called historical novel there is often considerable factual content. The author usually writes his story about imaginary characters against a background of actual men and events, or, sometimes, about real characters involved in fictional activities. In many cases much historical research has gone into the novel (see Edmonds 1936), and the factual content may be very high. For example, the *Harvard Guide to American History* (Handlin *et al.* 1966:237ff) recommends over 150 titles of American historical novels to professional historians. To sift out the fact from the fanciful, however, will often require going back to the source material.

There are cases, too, in which novels, short stories, and plays are indispensable. One such case is in the study of societies, mainly in the communist world, where fieldwork, firsthand observation, or archival study is difficult or impossible. In the study of Soviet society, for example, the economic historian Alexander Gerschenkron points out (Inkeles and Geiger 1961:395) that industrial and collective farm novels are valuable and unique sources for the study of the economic structure. There are certainly problems in using these sources, though not usually the problem of extreme subjectivity or individual orientation which one encounters in Western literature. The major concern is the degree to which the literature has been shaped by official propaganda and constrained by censorship. Gerschenkron's point is that although official policing is very significant, it is still possible to get a realistic picture. As an example, he cites from the *Kolkhoz* literature how farm managers evade government regulations on grain distribution. Various reasons contribute to the gaps in censorship, notably the need to present a credible picture to the reading public and the literary ploy of describing a conflict situation prior to its successful, official resolution. Such literature can help in interpreting the existing ethnographic and sociological sources (see, for example, E. Dunn and S. Dunn 1967).

Officially, restricted-access situations are not just confined to the communist world. Many countries in Afro-Asia are suspicious of the pure research objectives of Western scholars, partly as a result of a number of unfortunate, well-known, and highly publicized cases of the use of sociological knowledge for political objectives. In addition there are also many societies in the Western world in which there are strict rules of privacy which the field researcher, survey worker, or historian cannot penetrate. In all these cases literature is an important research aid.

Transient Documents

Although official, institutional, and private papers form the vast bulk of likely data, there are, in an age when increasing amounts of data are recorded, other possible sources. Some of these are published or reproduced mechanically but have only a limited circulation or life span so that they can only be found in archives or libraries. One important category of such transient documents is newspapers, which in many areas have a considerable time depth. The first newspapers are said to be found in ancient Rome or China, but important circulations did not occur until after the invention of the printing press in the fifteenth century. The first news consisted of descriptions of specific events such as royal occasions, wars, earthquakes, or sensational crimes (Bennett 1952:135), but newspapers as we know them were common by the end of the sixteenth century. Even magazines may have a time span of several hundred years; material from seventeenth-century magazines has been successfully utilized by sociologists.

Major political and economic events are particularly well covered in newspapers and have been widely used by historians. As W. I. Thomas and F. Znaniecki (1958) have shown, these sources also have a wide range of sociological relevance. In addition to specific articles and reports, there is valuable information in the classified sections (for example, births, deaths, and marriages), in announcements and reports of social and recreational activities or association meetings, in specialized sections dealing with social problems, in reports of court cases, and even in such unlikely places as letters to the editor (which may reveal important attitudinal traits) or the personal column.

The research worker should, in fact, look at the whole range of mass media (radio, television, movies, magazines, and so forth) now pervading not only Western society but also almost the entire world, including most parts of Afro-Asia, and providing direct reportage on, or indirect insights into, this society. It may well be that facts presented on television or in a glossy magazine or newspaper could not have been gathered by the fieldworker, even if he had the means to visit the villages or people concerned. For example, during my work in Switzerland I met many people who are very reluctant to discuss problems with a research worker, even if he is Swiss. Yet these same people open up completely for local or foreign television or magazine reporters.

Significant also are pamphlets, brochures, magazines, and broadsheets. These documents may yield data on the organizations responsible for publication (constitutions, policies, membership rosters, and so forth) and their particular fields of interest. Anthropologists and sociologists are increasingly coming to realize the importance of what have been called "associations," that is, institutions in which affiliation is voluntary, and often distinct from kinship or occupational affiliations. Most of the handouts of this category emanate from a multitude of associations (trade unions, political parties, church groups, clubs, and such) which are already well known in the Western world but which have also proliferated throughout Afro-Asia in recent years and whose activities embrace the countryside as well as the town.

Finally, pamphlets and newspapers especially may be a means for the research worker to keep in touch during the period when he has left the field but is still interested in ongoing processes, most notably political changes.

Further relevant sources, particularly in the study of European and North American societies, are directories and guides. In Switzerland, for example, the telephone directory contains not only information on the subscriber's occupation but also the maiden names of the women. Street directories, who's who's, official directories, and the like, obtainable from local libraries, also yield valuable data. The list of possible sources among the mountain of paper produced increasingly in all the world societies is endless. Sociologists (see, for example, Webb *et al.* 1966) have suggested that there is even a use for such seemingly unlikely pieces of paper as stamps, currency, mail-order catalogs, and supermarket bills. While there is probably a law of diminishing returns at some point in the paper chase, significant pieces of specific information may be obtained from these unlikely source materials. Similarly, the sources of the so-called auxilliary historical sciences (genealogy, epigraphy, cryptography, heraldry, and so forth) may occasionally be useful (see, for example, Samaran 1961).

Local Sources and Opinions

One very great drawback to most of the archives we have described, certainly in Afro-Asian areas, is the one-sidedness of the record, especially in the early days of contact. Travelers, missionaries, and administrators may have written voluminous reports, but seldom do local people themselves express their point of view voluntarily or without inhibition. The parallel problem in sociology and social history is to locate sources from the perspective of the great masses of society who do not leave a written record or who are inarticulate.

In many cases the early reporters did not have the necessary objectivity, linguistic skills, or cultural knowledge, even if they had the interest and sympathy, to record the local point of view. For example, Spicer (1962:21ff) found, when researching for his important study of culture contact among Indians of the Southwest, that only a very sketchy idea of the Indian interpretation and viewpoint could be obtained in the period before anthropological research. When they do exist, these "local sources," as we shall call them here, are of very great value to the research worker.

A likely spot for local sources is in those archives in which there is verbatim or direct reporting. The most common place for this reporting is in court and judicial records. For example, in his study of the Indians of the Southwest, Spicer uses court archives in which are recorded court appearances by Indians testifying against missionaries on charges of mistreatment or against civil governors on charges brought by the missionaries or themselves answering charges of insubordination or insurrection. Again, in the Pacific islands the evidence in land court records has been used to some effect in analyzing the social structure (Pitt 1970, France 1969) at different points in recent history.

These kinds of records are important not only because they preserve the direct comments of local participants but also because they throw light on critical issues in the social situation. In the judicial process of collecting and assessing evidence the relative rights of persons in regard to other persons and property, that is, the ideal social structure, is clarified. For example, Kai Erikson (1966), in his study of deviance in seventeenth-century Massachusetts, uses the court records of the witchcraft trials to analyze the boundary between normality and deviance in this society.

The major drawback to the use of this locally originating evidence is simply that it is not always a true representation of local opinion. The court situation, the language, the status and authority differences between court official and witnesses, and the interpretation where evidence is summarized rather than reported verbatim may all hinder spontaneous expression. For example, a major source for Fijian social history is the records of the Native Land Commission, which considered evidence on land tenure from 1880 to 1965 (France 1969) as part of the British administration's attempt to retain as much as possible of Fijian society in its pristine, traditional form. However, court procedure was based on English law-court precedents which were not well understood by Fijian witnesses. According to Fijian informants (Cato 1951), witnesses did not tell the truth because of fear of the high dignitaries who chaired the meetings or in order to enhance the prestige of the speakers' social group or to acquire property belonging to others. The interpretation of the evidence was based on the officials' belief that the social structure throughout Fiji resembled that of a particular district (Bau). Unfortunately, those locally originating documents in which spontaneity is more apparent (for example, letters, diaries) have a low rate of survival and are not nearly as plentiful, or as relevant to critical social issues, as the judicial records.

Local sources of this kind not only throw light on the past but also help in the interpretation of the present. The past is part of the present in the sense that all peoples interpret, and even validate, the present in terms of the past, real or imagined (Cunnison 1959, Sturtevant 1966:22ff). In some cultures this "folk history," as Sturtevant calls it (1966:22), is an explanation or a justification for most aspects of the social structure. Many Indian communities in the United States, for example, explain their separation from neighboring communities in terms of traditions, real or putative, about relations with the larger society. One tribe, the Lumbee of North Carolina, insists that they are derived from descendants of Raleigh's lost colony at Roanoke, (though there is no supporting evidence for this), while other tribes explain their isolation in terms of mistreatment, broken treaties and promises, and so forth.

Map, Pictorial, and Sound Archives

So far we have considered documents in which there are verbal written representations of facts. There are also documents in which there are cartographic or pictorial representations, sometimes in association with verbal representations. Maps are a most important category of nonverbal documents. Problems in the use of maps are similar in many ways to those in the use of verbal documents. Maps are probably easier to locate. Old maps have long been collectors' items, and there are important collections and catalogs. The Library of Congress, the British Museum, the Bibliotheque Nationale in France, and the various national geographical societies have very large collections.

Maps date back to the times of earliest manuscripts, though until the seventeenth century, many maps contained fanciful representations of mythical countries, continents, and contours, like the Strait of Anian, the southern land mass of "Beach," and so on. More accurate maps were made by the early explorers. Accuracy was stimulated by the political and diplomatic needs for determining boundaries. Much detail in early maps, especially in North America, came as a result of economic development. Here, groups like the Hudson Bay Company and the North West Company provided much information and even employed full-time cartographers (Handlin et al. 1966:69). Later, map making became an important function of government departments and official agencies.

These early maps contain much information other than the physical features of the countryside. Many early maps of the American Indian territories, for example (see Gunnerson 1957), show population movement, indicating also number and size of settlements and occasionally including ethnographic notes as well. There are very important maps from the colonial era showing land use, land boundaries (cadastral maps), communications, and so forth, or the areal distribution of statistics derived from censuses or other surveys. Especially in Europe and North America in the modern period, an ever-widening range of data of a social nature has appeared on maps, not only vital statistics but also data relating to such topics as religion, ethnicity, health, education, and distribution of wealth.

Mention should be made as well of the sources from which many modern printed maps are made, that is, air photo mosaics. If the mosaics are available over a time period, they provide a valuable record of changing spatial distributions: land expansion, changing crop patterns or land use, population density, communications, and the like. Sometimes they may furnish revealing facts which are not readily observed on the ground.

There are, admittedly, considerable problems involved in interpreting maps, especially old manuscript maps. Dates are often misleading, as copies were frequently made that included new information. Falsification was also prevalent until the nineteenth century. In the early maps information was often based on heresay or legend, and the maps showed fictitious physical features, while positions or distances were not measured according to accurate surveying specifications. In general, ethnographic information on such maps is also likely to be suspect.

Pictorial records consist of documents either drawn by hand or photographed. These visual records, especially photographs, have a great value in anthropological research (Collier 1967), recording minutiae which can easily evade the fieldworker's scrutiny. Drawings and paintings also have a value. Although recording subjectively, this selectivity throws light on contemporary attitudes and conventions. For example, caricatures and cartoons not only illustrate shifting conceptions of humor but reveal much about social customs, especially political attitudes, as well.

Like maps, pictorial records are relatively easy to locate since prints, paintings, drawings, and such are collected and are of public interest. There are important photographic collections in the great archives and libraries, such as the National Archives or Library of Congress, or in special collections such as the Museum of Modern Art in New York, while paintings are to be found in major museums and galleries.

Finally, the research worker should not ignore verbal but unwritten documents, preserved on record and tape in sound archives, containing material which may not be in the written documentary record.

Statistics

Pictorial or cartographic documents are not the only kind of nonverbal representation. There are also vast collections of numerical data in contemporary archives. Statistics were first collected by governments to help in such tasks as customs or tax collections, or fixing political representation. For example, in the United States (Handlin et al. 1966:27) there are customs and census figures from the late eighteenth century. To these were added in the nineteenth-century figures on such activities as manufactures, occupations, mines, agriculture, commerce, illiteracy, insanity, pensioners, libraries, newspapers, and crime. There were similar trends in Europe. The collection of statistics became an important part of governmental activities in the colonial and developing world as well, especially as ideas of projective planning became popular.

Because statistics are generally gathered under official aegis, they are to be found mainly in the public archives, relevant government departments, or special statistical or census departments. Access to official statistical materials is usually less restrictive than documentary access, for anonymity can be assured by numerical representation. However, the individual sources of these generalizations, of most interest to the microcosmic researcher, are highly restricted. Legislation assuring anonymity is an important means of securing information from citizens. Census documents in the United States, for example, have a seventy-two year limit. Statistics are, however, to be found in a wide range of institutions outside official circles. Industrial, commercial, agricultural, professional, labor, educational, religious, political, welfare, and similar organizations are constantly gathering figures, though, especially in commercial organizations, access is often very restricted. There are also specialized statistical organizations, such as the American Statistical Association, or research bureaus, like the National Bureau of Economic Research or the Brookings Institute, entirely devoted to statistical activities covering a very wide field. The development of the computer and electronic data processing has greatly aided statistical collection.

There are many problems peculiar to the interpretation of statistical documentation. In the early days there were very great problems of assessing and comparing enumeration techniques, as data collection was haphazard. Even when, in the late nineteenth century, sampling procedures based on the calculus of probability were introduced, there still remained the problem of relating the statistical abstractions to the more specific descriptions of verbal documents. It was this difficulty which contributed in large measure to the reluctance of many historians to utilize statistical data (Handlin *et al.* 1966:26). These difficult problems will be returned to when interpretation is discussed in detail (Chapter 4).

Data Banks

Documents, maps, and statistics must usually be consulted *in situ*, in the archives or collections where they have been deposited, but increasingly there are copies or summaries available in places which may be more accessible. Many of the large libraries and archives in North America have microfilms, microcards, or microfiches of important documents relating to particular areas, which may be loaned out. There are also an increasing number of data files, archives, and banks, mainly in North America, containing summaries or computer tapes of documentary and published material, particularly statistical data. In addition these data banks may contain the results of their own surveys or summaries of surveys which are not easily obtainable elsewhere.

For the anthropologist the Human Relations Area Files are an important source of comparative material, consisting mainly of rare published material, though there are only a few machine-readable files. Particular theoretical interests or surveys of particular areas may be served by files from the larger data banks (see Council of Social Science Data Archives 1967, Rokkan 1966). Historians interested in quantitative problems are currently making extensive use of such sources, especially in the political and economic fields (see Dollar and Jensen 1970). Many institutions are also building up microfilm collections of archives specifically oriented to anthropological or sociological interests. One example is the recent project of the American Philosophical Society to film and survey relevant documents from the Archivos de Indias in Seville, Spain.

Further Reading

The *Historian's Handbook* (Wood Gray *et al.* 1964) provides a useful and brief guide to the sources of historical data. Beginning in the library, the student should consult the major printed catalogs of published works such as those of the Library of Congress, the British Museum, National Union, and the Bibliotheque Nationale, which are indexed by both author and subject. Of particular value also is the *London Bibliography of the Social Sciences* (1931–62), produced by the London School of Economics, as well as the annual UNESCO sociology and anthropology bibliographies. An excellent bibliography of bibliographies has been prepared by T. Besterman (1964–1966). Periodicals are covered in the *Reader's Guide to Periodical Literature* and the union list of serials published by H. W. Wilson Company of New York, as well as in the Library of Congress lists. Major newspapers such as the London *Times* and the New York *Times* have their own indexes, and there is also a union list for North America (H. W. Wilson Company) and the Commonwealth (Hewitt 1960). There are lists of encyclopedia directories, biographies, who's who's, and other research aids in Winchell's (1967) guide.

Henderson (1957 *et seq.*) is more specifically concerned with directories. For biographies there are the *Biography Index* and the *Current Biography Yearbook* published by H. W. Wilson Company or Michaud's *Biographie Universelle*. There is an excellent list of sources and research aids in Dollar and Jensen (1970), particularly for the United States. A very good guide to American sources generally is provided by Handlin and associates (1966), while Webb and associates (1966) provide a wide coverage of sociological interests with an excellent bibliography.

For particular areas important bibliographies and guides are those by Taylor (1965) (South Pacific); Fürer-Haimendorf (1958–1964) (Southeast Asia); Freeman and Smith (1966) (American Indian); Hewitt (1957) (British Commonwealth); and Ford (1956) (Africa). The International African Institute publishes its card indexes (Africa Bibliography series), and there are important lists for Asia in the *Journal of Asian Studies*.

Guides for the world's major public archives have been prepared by Galbraith (1952) for the British Public Record Office and Hamer (1961) for the United States. Other relevant archival guides are those compiled by Ghose (1963) (India) and Gomez Canedo (1961) (Latin America). Useful guides to government publications are those by Ford and Ford (1955) and E. S. Brown (1950). For manuscript collections reference should be made to the work of Downs and Jenkins (1967). The guide by Handlin and his associates (1966) has full lists and bibliographies.

Of special interest to anthropologists working in archives are the London University West African History Guides (Carson 1965, 1968; Gray and Chambers 1965; Ryder 1965). Although concerned with a narrow regional area, these volumes in fact indicate the major colonial and other archives in the European countries. A similar function is served by Marchant's (1966) guide to the Protestant missionaries in China.

A good guide to statistical sources is provided by Dollar and Jensen (1970), and also worth consulting are the books by Wasserman (1962 *et seq.*), Adriot (1961), and E. S. Brown (1950). Bowles (1967) has edited a valuable collection of studies on computer uses in fields including history.

Many of the famous exploration and mission accounts have been published. A most important series is the Hakluyt volumes, which are mainly exploration literature but which include some missionary works as well. A most important missionary source is *The Jesuit Relations* (1896–1901), in which accounts of the travels and explorations of the Jesuit missionaries in the seventeenth and eighteenth century are printed in 73 volumes. Important works of individual missionaries include those by Lescarbot (1907–1914), Lafitau (1839), Dobritzhofer (1822), Charlevoix (1900) (North America); Ellis (1828, 1939–1942), Gill (1876), Turner (1861, 1884), Strehlow (1907–1920), Codrington (1891) (South Pacific); Callaway (1868–1870), Livingstone (1963), Junod (1912–1913), Roscoe (1911), E. W. Smith (1920) (Africa); and Huc (1852, 1855) (Asia). Many of these volumes are now being republished by the reprint companies. One interesting series which includes 100 volumes of works by missionaries, explorers, administrators, traders, and so forth, is the March of America series published by University Microfilms of Ann Arbor. Further bibliographical information can be found in the *Bibliotheca Missionum*, published by the *Intenationales Institut für Missionwissenschaffliche* (for the Catholic missions) and in Barrow's (1955) bibliography.

The writings of administrators are not as valuable as mission accounts, but an interesting example is the work of Yoe (1963), the detailed description of Burmese society by Sir J. G. Scott, who spent thirty-five years in the country.

Beyond the public and mission archives the search is much more difficult, especially for the private papers, though there are guides for some countries—for example, the United States (Hamer 1961) and Great Britain (Historical Manuscripts Commission 1956). There are also usually published lists of the holdings of universities, museums, libraries, and other scholarly institutions, though the research worker often has to know where material is likely to be found beforehand. Parker (1944) and Hepworth (1966) indicate procedures in local history searches, while guides to special fields are provided by Doane (1960) (genealogy) and Goldstein (1964) (folklore).

For business and commercial records, there are directories to the business houses in most countries, and most maintain their own archives. For secondary material there is no substitute for the Baker Library of Business History at Harvard. A useful bibliography has been compiled by Larson (1948). Cantril (1947) has written what is still a very useful introduction to opinion polls. W. I. Thomas and F. Znaniecki (1958) provide many examples of the use of letters; another interesting example of this form has been provided by Kartini (1964).

For maps there are the catalogs of the Library of Congress and British Museum, while L. A. Brown (1949) has compiled a bibliography of cartographic literature. There is a list of sources on pictorial and sound records in the guide by Handlin *et al.* (1966:65ff, 245), while Collier (1967) outlines the anthropological uses. There is also an excellent guide to the historical uses of fiction and a bibliography in the guide by Handlin and associates (1966:237).

Microcopy sources are listed in Hale's (1961) guide, while the Council of Social Science Data Archives (1967) describes the data banks. Rokkan (1966) provides useful additional descriptions and discussions.

3

Reaching and Recording Data

Gaining Access

HAVING SURVEYED the probable range of sources, the researcher now has the problem of extracting relevant data. First, access must be secured to the sources. In the case of libraries and public archives there is not usually a great problem, though there is always an etiquette of admission and use which should be stringently observed. Most public archives ask for letters of identity, some insist that identity cards or visas with passport photos are carried at all times, and most, like the Public Record Office in England, have special rules, such as the stipulation that only pencils be used for recording.

Nonpublic archives, that is, archives for which there is not statutory provision for access and use, pose different kinds of problems. In anthropological fieldwork access can often be tied in with the fieldwork protocol. The official letters and credentials which the anthropologist carries, or the officials who are concerned with arranging the fieldwork, may be enough to secure access.

In general, officials in the various archives are willing to help if they can, though there are always confidential files, or officials who have a deep-seated suspicion that the academic is an iconoclast whose main function is to discredit the establishment. In some cases it will be up to the anthropologist or sociologist, as, indeed, it is in fieldwork situations, to establish enough rapport with officials to allow consultation of files. In all cases the research worker must be aware of the conventions and rituals that are part of the official establishment and the official conception of archive use.

In particular, there is usually a very important difference between the academic and the officials' use of data. The academic descriptions and analyses are, potentially at least, public knowledge. Villages, towns, cities, and characters are real places and people, usually easily recognized, even if they carry pseudonyms. However, much official data is for internal use and consultation, and is only revealed publicly in carefully guarded communiqués or anonymous statistics. In some cases this is because the record is frank, discrediting, or libelous, or potentially valuable to third parties, or because it was divulged only on the assumption that it would remain confidential. Use of these files, if allowed, may involve the research worker in a commitment not to publish certain facts, not to quote sources, or in official censorship. Despite these restrictions, confidential data, especially in the local files, may provide important insights not easily acquired elsewhere. Occasionally, it will be possible to circumvent the restrictions by convincing officialdom of the unimportance of publishing this or that closed fact.

A further problem which arises in connection with the consultation of local archives during anthropological fieldwork is the effect of consultation on rapport in the fieldwork village. In many cases the anthropologist is introduced into a community through official channels, and whatever he does, there remains, at least in some peoples' minds, the suspicion that he has an official connection and purpose. This purpose may be thought to be beneficial (for example, investigation of the village for development aid or the like), but more often it will be assumed that the anthropologist has a detrimental purpose, that he is, for example, an income tax inspector or a foreign agent. Such an assumption may be bolstered if it is widely known that the researcher spends time in the archives, and rapport with villagers may subsequently be harmed.

Research Aids

Once access having been gained, the next problem is to reach and record relevant data. Here, too, many of the techniques employed by the historian can be very useful. An important number of research aids can be used before, or during, archival research. First, there are in relation to the larger archives, published catalogs, guides, bibliographies, and check lists, as well as general works of reference (almanacs, calendars, yearbooks, directories, atlases, who's who's, biographies, registers, encyclopedias, and so forth) relating to the area of interest. In addition many of the larger archives have detailed inventories, catalogs, indexes, lists, abstracts, and summaries of their holdings. For example, the Public Record Office in London has three large rooms containing 14,000 volumes of indexes to part of its holdings.

Beyond and in addition to this, it is necessary to draw on the expertise and knowledge of the library and archival staff or of other specialists. One of the by-products, in fact, of working especially in smaller archives is meeting specialists who may have similar areal or subject interests and who may be able to put the researcher on the track of relevant material. Skillful use of these aids is essential to historical research, greatly shortening the time spent in searching for documentary evidence.

Recording Data

Historians' techniques in the recording of data are also useful, though the essential techniques are similar to the recording of fieldwork facts. The important aim is to secure a fast, accurate, economical record of data that is easily retrievable. The record should be flexible to permit rearrangement when the material is being written up. One of the faults of some nineteenth-century historians was that the record, made in the form of a book of transcriptions and abstracts, reflected the organization of the sources from which they worked (Handlin *et al.* 1966: 39). This reflection inevitably colored the subsequent narrative or analysis. For most purposes some kind of simple, written card index system or indexed notebook is adequate. Some researchers keep biographical as well as subject cards and less often summary cards.

For statistical or quantitative data, especially, the record should be in machine-readable form such as punched cards. Although historians are currently doing some research into computer development and information retrieval, few archives have facilities for computerized research, and it will probably be necessary to import any equipment for such facilities.

Photocopying methods are probably more important for the anthropologist and sociologist. Facilities for photocopying are widely available, or portable equipment can be used. Photocopy, either microfilm, microfiche, or direct copy, is most useful when relevant data are concentrated and not easily summarized, as in maps or census materials. However, as in the tape recording of oral fieldwork data, photocopying records too much data and is not usually a substitute for a careful and selective sifting of the archival record.

In fact, a key problem at this stage of research is, usually, to survey and record only that information which is relevant since the sources almost always contain much more information than is needed. The researcher must develop an aptitude for scanning sources for important information, a skill that is not usually needed in fieldwork. Selectivity is helped by the intelligent use of indexes, but in addition the researcher must be able to recognize relevant information and documents of critical importance quickly. It may even be that one document or file contains most of the relevant material (see, for example, M. G. Smith 1960).

Annotation and Indexing

There is one important difference between the recording of archival and fieldwork data. It is a convention in historical research that the source of each piece of information or quotation is precisely noted, and quoted when the work is written up. This means that in addition to files of content notes, it is necessary to keep a classified card index of sources. This is a research aid in itself in that it makes the task of going back to archival material or cross-checking much easier.

There are few problems in the case of published sources which may be recorded as in the standard bibliography. Unpublished archival material must be handled differently. In the United States there is a standard entry form for public documents printed by the Library of Congress, but most archival document entries have not been standardized and there is no standard form of citation. Source cards, however, should record the full title of the source, relevant dates, file numbers, the form of script (for example, manuscript, typescript, or mimeograph), the size of the collection, and its present location. Sources may be classified chronologically, alphabetically, geographically, or systematically, that is, by subject or source. Many historians (see, for example, Handlin *et al.* (1966:42ff) separate out primary (that is, generally firsthand) from secondary sources and classify further under headings such as manuscripts, pamphlets, public documents, and newspapers. The most useful method is probably the alphabetical—especially if there are a large number of sources. Sources may be arranged as in the conventional bibliography, in alphabetical order by the author's name, if the record is under his signature, or under the name of the organizational author, the institution to which the record pertains. Some historians classify by the first letter in the title of the document.

> Maxwell, W., 1848, Information Regarding
> the Islands of the Samoan Group.
> Great Britain, Foreign Office,
> FO 58/63/232-54-MS, Public Record
> Office, London.

Example 1a. Author entry

> Foreign Office, Great Britain, Manuscript
> Reports. 1. Information Regarding
> the Islands of the Samoan Group,
> 1848 (Maxwell, W.), FO 58/63/232-54,
> Public Record Office, London.

Example 1b. Institution entry

Signed entries in the organization record are usually recorded under the organization, and the person's name noted if relevant or important. Often within an institution, such as a mission society or a government colonial office, there will be a large number of categories of records, different kinds of records, or separate series. These different categories may again be ordered alphabetically and within the category according to the file number.

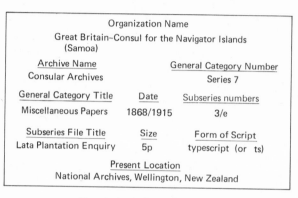

Example 2. Source format

In some cases, especially in local records, there may not be file numbers, in which case the items can be ordered alphabetically, by date, or as they occur *in situ* in the record, though the point should be made that the annotation is of the author's creation.

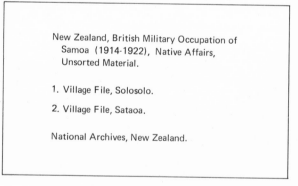

Example 3. In-situ entry

Each source entry does not require a separate source card, unless this is the only source entry for the institution, in which case the date and title of the document can be put after the institution, finishing with the series and file numbers. If there are multiple entries for an institution, it is usual to have a card for each class of document (as classified by. the archives) and to record sub-categories and series consulted.

New Zealand, Island Territories Department
   Archives.

National Archives, New Zealand.

Series 1.   Registered Files.

Series 2.   Samoan Affairs.

Series 3.   Legal.

Series 4.   Accounts.

Series 5.   Customs and Taxes . . . , etc.

Example 4. Source categories: Card 1

New Zealand — Island Territories Department.

Miscellaneous Office Papers, National Archives,
   New Zealand.

1. Documentary Record of the Lauati Rebellion,
   1909

3. Reports on the Mau Rebellion, 1935-1936

13. Vailima Conference on Education, 1946 . . . , etc.

Example 4. Source categories: Card 2

In annotating in the content cards or file, or later in footnoting, it is advisable to have some form of shorthand reference to the record, especially if there is much repetition. Author entries can be handled conventionally, using name, year, page, and so on. For institutional entries, relevant first letters may be used together with file numbers. Example 2 could then become GBC7/3e (that is, Great Britain, Consul, and so forth). An alternative is to use key works (in our example, Great Britain, Consul, Navigator Islands 7/3e, or, if following previous references, Ibid., 7/3). For some records which have a regularity over time (for example, newspapers, official gazettes, and journals), it is usual to simply note the name and place of publication together with the actual date and page number. Court cases and legal records have special and complex rules of citation, but in general the former are referred to by quoting the names of the plaintiff and defendant and the place where the case is reported, while laws are referred to by quoting the title, date, statute and number, and so forth.

An additional aid used in many archives and libraries is to develop an annotated subject catalog indexed, usually, by names, places, and important occurrences, and so forth. These kinds of cards are especially useful for personal or unsorted papers for which there has not been an adequate filing or indexing system.

Newell, Rev. John E., 1852-1910.

The Samoan papers (1881-1910) (1881-1887, Savai'i; 1887-1910, Malua) of the Rev. Newell, containing biographical details, sermons, pamphlets, diaries, notes, and correspondence. Letters contain details on the relationship of the missions with Samoan chiefs and people, and with government traders, etc. Notes and diaries contain detailed descriptions on Samoan society and language.

I Trunk, London Missionary Society, Livingstone House, London, England.

Example 5. Main card for collection

On the cards are general descriptions of the subject matter in the holdings. There is, first of all, a general card (Example 5) outlining the major contents of the collection, though, of course, in the case of large collections there will be a number of these general cards. Following this card are the added subject entries in alphabetical order preceded by a listing. These added entries contain, like the general cards, details of subject matter in the holdings. Subject cards also contain location data or references back to the main classification. Examples 6 and 7 are of annotated subject cards:

Malua, Samoa.

Newell, Rev. John E., 1852-1910.

Letters (1887-1910) describing the running of the mission seminary at Malua and staff and students from the villages. Reports (1890-1903) to Mission Head— quarters. Diaries (1888-1910) with descriptions of mission life.

Example 6. Added entry card—place

Moran, Cardinal P.

Newell, Rev. John E., 1852-1910

Replies (1899-1900) to Cardinal Moran's letters attacking the work of LMS missionaries in Samoa, also printed in various newspapers (1899- 1900, *Sydney Daily Telegraph, The Sydney Morning Herald, Manchester Guardian*).

Example 7. Added entry card—persons

There are also special indexes, for example, of names or periods, which are useful aids. Another form of indexing, common in many archives, is calendaring. In this method documents are ordered chronologically and a summary of the document's contents included. Calendaring saves a good deal of time in going back to the documents. However, most researchers have only limited time at their disposal, and a law of diminishing returns sets in at some stage. For most purposes the source index can be a simple list.

Classification schemes for pictorial or cartographic materials are very similar to document classification, being indexed by name, place, author, subject matter, or chronologically. Each item should have its own card containing, in addition to the above items, scale, size, number of insets, and so forth. For printed maps there are standard Library of Congress forms.

Personal Archives

Despite efforts to restrict the size of the record, many historical researchers find that they are collecting an archive in their own right. It is often easier and quicker in the collecting stage of research to buy the relevant documents, reports, newspapers, and so forth, for later analysis and referral. In the age of photocopying most researchers acquire copies of key documents from distant archives.

It is essential at this stage to ensure efficient storage and retrieval, and a small outlay of equipment and time saves much time later on in the project. However, maximum flexibility must still be retained. In general, documents are most efficiently stored according to their size. Down to the middle of the nineteenth century, many documents, especially letters, and the like, were put in folders or parcels and wrapped up. Many archives nowadays use vertical filing, and this is most useful for the amateur archive as well. A filing cabinet or large drawer suffices for quarto or larger material below about twenty pages, while clippings or smaller items should be pasted on quarto or foolscap sheets. Larger collections of documents are better stapled or bound together, or put in file boxes on open shelving. Similarly, microfilms, microfiches, data decks, slides, tapes, and so forth, can be stored on open shelves or in special smaller filing cabinets. Newspapers, large maps, charts, and the like are best stored in larger folders or covers in horizontal drawers or positions. The contents of all files, folders, and boxes should be clearly labeled. In addition, tapes or photographic materials should, if possible, have the label included on the material itself.

Ideally, all material should be indexed in a master card box or file as it comes in and preferably annotated so as to describe subject matter. In general, classification should be open ended, new files being opened as new subject matter is obtained, and it is usually better to have categories too small rather than too big. Files can be alphabetically ordered, though most archives have a combination systematic (that is, by subject) and numerical system, but ordering is not usually by author, as in the libraries. It is usual when files are derived from other archives or collections to retain the classification system of the original or to retain the documents in the form in which they were originally held (*respect des fonds*). Sometimes, however, material may be hopelessly jumbled or documents may have been produced over time without classification. Such files can be ordered in any logical way, probably best by the institutions producing the material and then by a numerical sequence based on the sequence of the arrival of the documents into the collection. Where there is a chronological sequence, filing should be seriatim and indexed by date. In all other cases, every page in the file should be numbered.

The major point throughout, however, is to keep the system flexible and adapted to the particular needs of the research project. Once again, a law of diminishing returns sets in at some point as far as time invested in the project is concerned.

Manuscript Preservation and Processing

Most documents that the research worker acquires for his private archive may be preserved and used without any special attention. But it may be that documents will be acquired which need processing before data can be extracted from them. During fieldwork, for example, old documents may be acquired, or the researcher may be admitted to a previously untouched and unkempt archive. Especially in tropical countries, documents deteriorate quickly in the damp environment in which paper-eating bugs flourish.

In general, manuscript preservation is a job for the skilled expert, but some things may be done by the amateur. Great caution should be used in the repair of damaged documents. Many archives have been ruined by the use of cellophane tapes, and generally it is better not to mend a legible document. If mending is to be done, there are special tapes obtainable from the library supply houses. Crumbling documents are best processed by silking or lamination, a process in which a special gauze or cellulose foil is applied to the document. This is a job which certainly should be left to the expert.

Further Reading

Much of the reading on access is contained in those references mentioned in the last chapter dealing with source location, particularly guides to the archives. For some lighthearted comments on historians in archives, the student should read Cohn's (1962) article. Similarly, the major research aids which are as vital in the recording as in the searching stage have been mentioned. Barzun and Graff (1962) have prepared a most useful manual for all aspects of historical research, with many details on recording, annotation, and so forth. There is much useful material in the historical methodology literature, for example, the works of Hockett (1955), Gottschalk (1969), and Garraghan and Delanglez (1946). On specific topics there are the works of Dow (1924) on note systems and Carey (1951) on indexes.

Important books on archive organization and the handling of documents are those by Jenkinson (1965), Bordin and Warner (1966), and Schellenberg (1965). Mechanized sources are dealt with by Vickery (1961). Much important literature can also be found in occasional or periodical publications such as the bulletins of the National Archives, the *American Archivist,* and *Archivum,* the annual journal of the International Council on Archives. The last two journals provide important bibliographies from time to time.

4

The Critical Analysis of Documentary Evidence

S O FAR I have considered what documents the researcher may find useful, and how he may extract information from them. The next, and difficult, task is to analyze and interpret the data. This involves at the outset a number of practical problems. The research worker has to be fully aware of the limits of the kind of evidence he has extracted from the historical record, and particularly the ways in which this evidence compares and differs from data gathered in fieldwork, or from other kinds of sources. This is an essential preliminary to utilizing and integrating historical data into analyses.

Establishing Probabilities

One obvious difference between historical and fieldwork data is that the latter has usually been gathered by the fieldworker himself. It is firsthand observation, whereas in the historical record the perspective is through somebody else's eyes (primary sources), and information may even be gathered by third or fourth hand (secondary sources). This means that the anthropologist or sociologist using historical documents has to go to some lengths to establish what has been called the "framework of facts," that is, events, incidents, or structural features, and so forth, for which there is a high degree of probability. The research worker cannot go back himself to those events reported; he must rely, therefore, on his ability to evaluate the statements that have been made about the situation. Thus the first concern must be with those factors likely to affect the veracity of these statements.

Before going on, I should emphasize the importance of probability in the framework of fact. In the nineteenth and early twentieth centuries may historians followed Ranke's dictum that the historian's purpose was "simply to show how it really was" (*wie es eigentlich gewesen*), that is, to provide an accurate compilation of past events. It was assumed that there existed some kind of hard core of indisputable facts. Since the late nineteenth century, however, there has been a strong reaction against the Rankian scissors-and-paste history. Many historians have argued that the nature of the facts depends on the interpretation of the historian himself, and some have gone so far as to say that history is quite subjective and that the history of the same events is rewritten by every generation. However, most historians recognize that although there is always a subjective and contemporaneous viewpoint, interpretation rests ultimately on an interaction between the facts, as they probably happened, the historical observer, and the historian's thoughts and present situation (Collingwood 1945, Carr 1964:21). I will return to this important triangle later.

The job of assessing the probability of these kinds of "facts" and the statements made about them is the researcher's initial major task. There are several basic steps in this process.

First, an assessment must be made of how far the document represents an accurate description of the situation, that is, the degree to which the statement about the facts agrees with the facts as they probably happened. To begin with, the research worker must know the details of the document's authorship, the date and place of the events described, and the date when and place where the description was written up. He should try to find out details about the context of the author's observations and recording, the events that were going on around and before the event described and recorded. Necessary, too, is a knowledge of details about the author's life, his attitudes and experiences, and the like. Finally, the research worker must know whether the document is the original description or analysis. If it is not the original, then details on the intermediaries and the circumstances of communication should be known. The job of establishing the physical authenticity of a document is often called external criticism. The analysis of the contents to detect inconsistencies, errors, or falsehoods is the process of internal criticism. Both external and internal criticism play a part in the third and most essential job of evaluation, that is, weighing up the evidence at hand, not only trying to assess more fine degrees of reliability but also interpreting statements, trying to say, that is, what the "evidence" is evidence of (Handlin et al. 1966:23). To illustrate the problems involved in these processes, more detailed examples of critical procedures will now be considered.

Originality, Errors, and Falsification

The question of originality is not usually the most serious problem. The kinds of documents relevant to anthropological and sociological research are often the work of firsthand observers. There is not usually the problem, which occurs, for instance, in medieval historiography, of interpreting the fragmented, distorted, or inaccurate commentaries of a string of intermediaries. In many modern political and judicial institutions recording is done *in extenso* in shorthand.

Accidental error and falsification are common occurrences in the historical record. Historians over the years have developed a series of strict critical tests and guidelines for detecting these errors and falsities, either in originals or in copies.

The French historical methodologists Langlois and Seignobos (1898:76) have claimed that "texts degenerate in accordance with certain laws." In fact, most of those "laws" turn on reasonably obvious indications, such as confusion of sense in the document, internal inconsistencies, inconsistencies with known data or other reports, and so forth, nearness to the situation, pressures making for modification. In general, if the research worker is vigilant, skeptical, and well informed on the background to his document, most major errors can be detected.

Similarly, investigation of authorship is not likely to be as great a problem for the anthropologist or sociologist as it is for many historians. Most modern documents are likely to be signed, or, in the case of administration papers, at least initialed, though dating may be more of a problem.

Interpretation of Reporting—Preliminary Points

A much more significant problem is that historical documents are often summaries after the events and not detailed records of events as they occur. The differences between this aspect of fieldwork and historical data should not be over-emphasized, however. It is a difference of degree rather than kind. In fact, the fieldwork record resembles the historical record in important respects, and presents similar problems of verifying or establishing reliability. Many fieldworkers do not record events as they happen—often, in fact, the social situation precludes this—but write up their impressions at the first opportunity, probably, at best, several hours after the event. These notes inevitably contain summaries and abbreviations and may not be consulted again until the fieldworker is writing up his material. At this stage, connections and details which were apparent at the time the summary was written may have been forgotten. The fieldwork record has become, in a sense, a kind of historical document.

However, this time lapse may be much less than in historical writing. Reliability of evidence tends to decrease as the time lapse between the action and the reporting increases, though the human memory is a complex variable. The problem is not quite the same in social survey work. Many questionnaires are filled in on the spot by informants or interviewers. The data recorded, however, are often details of past actions, attitudes, beliefs, or events.

Another variable is the attentiveness of the witness at the time of the action. The story is told (Gottschalk 1945:39) of a psychology professor who started a brawl in his class and then asked the students to write an essay on what had happened. Apart from conflicting accounts, the most important feature of the reports was that nobody noticed that in the middle of the fracas the professor had taken a banana from his pocket, peeled it, and eaten it. Inattentiveness to boring but important detail is not only an historical observer's vice, as many anthropologists who have participated in exciting feasts and ceremonials well know.

In fieldwork also a considerable amount of evidence may come from second hand. Anthropologists try to be participant-observers, but they cannot participate in, or observe, everything. Sometimes the events in the field which the anthropologist wants to see occur simultaneously, and there are many relevant events which occur outside the restricted time–space framework of the fieldwork—or while the fieldworker is in some way incapacitated or otherwise occupied. Information related to these events or facts is gathered by research assistants or local informants. The anthropologist will, even when he is a participant-observer, utilize the ideas and interpretations of other people to help explain what is going on around him.

Similarly, in survey work, information is gathered by intermediary research assistants, often in terms of a highly structured questionnaire which does not allow the recording of unexpected or unwanted, but sometimes relevant, data.

As far as establishing the framework of fact is concerned, a more important difference than the relative proximity of the observer is his subjectivity. It is not that the anthropologist or sociologist is really objective in his selection and interpretation of data. His intellectual attitudes are the product of the conventions of a particular culture and a discipline, and he is constantly interpreting and translating the actuality of the fieldwork situations into these terms. The point is rather that these subjectivities remain substantially the same at the time of recording and analysis. Even if these attitudes undergo some radical change during or after fieldwork, there will presumably be some awareness of the bases of previous subjectivity. The research worker does not have the same knowledge of the subjectivity of those persons who produced the historical record.

The subjectivity in historical documents may well result in an undue concentration on certain features of the social structure, omission of facts which do not support the case being presented, or a willful distortion or invention of facts. The only, albeit partial, solution to this problem is for the anthropologist or sociologist to absorb as much of the relevant literature as he can so that he knows, to some degree, the reporter's frame of mind. For example, an anthropologist attempting to utilize mission records to any degree should read widely in the religious and social history of the period.

In addition, an assessment of the accuracy of a particular document can be achieved by looking critically at the subject matter of the document and its author (for example, is there an official line on the subject?), its intended circulation, its purpose (the most accurate documents are *aide-mémoires* and straight reports), its confidentiality (the more confidential it is, the more truthful it is likely to be), the personal position of the writer and his sympathies and antipathies (even such things as the state of his health), what, if anything, the author has to gain from a particular point of view, and so on. There are also certain conditions favorable to credibility (Gottschalk 1945:43), for example, when the witness is under legal oath, or fears retributions to himself or family for prevarication, or when he is indifferent to consequences and has little desire to please, displease, propogandize, and so forth, or when he has little to gain financially or otherwise, or when the facts are felt to be common knowledge. Finally, it may be possible to discover from other sources something of the writer's ability in, or reputation for, accurate reporting. Some writers are consistently inaccurate. This condition is known to the historians as "Froude's disease"—after the English historian who was "destined never to advance any statement that was not disfigured by error" (Langlois and Seignobos 1898:125). In fact, this condition is rather rare, and a writer's evidence should never be completely rejected because of his reputation but should rather be more carefully scrutinized.

Fortunately, the anthropologist or sociologist does not face the same problems of, for example, the medieval historian, who must be constantly on the lookout for false or missing documents. Most of the documents relevant to anthropological study are housed in secure archives, though local records are particularly likely to have been tampered with.

Bias

Very often the problem is not as simple as asking whether or not a given statement about a fact is true or false but rather is one of ascertaining the degree of bias in any statement. There can only be a complete record of any given event in a limited sense. For one thing, the semantic constraints in language itself do not allow the same kind of completeness in the documentary record as that recorded, for example, in a photograph or movie. Even in the visual record, the camera cannot be in all places at all times. There is always a viewpoint. In reporting there is always a bias, a priority in the order in which details are noted, a selectivity in impressions recorded, the choice of words, the tone of the writing, and a hundred other subtle points. It should be noted too that bias is not simply to be found in reportage, in the historical observers document, but enters, of course, into the research worker's interpretation and analysis. The first kind of bias I shall term "observer bias" and the second, "interpretational bias."

These comments apply as much to the collection of statistics as to qualitative data observation. Even in a random sample, the choice of sample units (for example, household, or persons), has some effect on the ultimate analysis. Much more significantly, most statistics are derived from verbal statements in questionnaires, or instructions to officials, and such, which involve the same kinds of problems as straight verbal recording. Admittedly, the informant does not have the range of reply to be found in unrestricted reports of statements, but the document is not free of bias for this reason. There is initially the interpretational bias of the person who constructed the questionnaire, and there are times when this is so great that information gathered is largely a reflection of the research worker's own models. Even in the most carefully constructed questionnaire, there is a degree of this reflected bias.

Individuality in reporting may in itself not greatly affect the value of the document, but there is a point at which the observer bias becomes relevant and may lead to the greater problems of error and distortion. In general, the investigation of observer bias proceeds in much the same way as the estimation of accuracy, the important factors being the background of the author, the context of the document, and so forth. Observer bias differs, however, from more sporadic inaccuracies in that it is more thoroughgoing and likely to color a major part of the reportage.

Similar comments can be made about interpretational bias. Some historians, such as Barzun and Graff (1957:160), go as far as to define this bias as the point at which the writers total interests spoil the objectivity of his analysis.

Interpretational bias can lead to radically different descriptions of situations, to what Norman Cantor (1968:73) has recently called the "Louis the Fat syndrome." Louis the Fat was an extremely inept French king of the twelfth century who, through obscure or confused references, was variously interpreted by historians as a hero-king repulsing a bad German emperor and founding the French monarchy or a bad king invading Flanders. Similarly, there are explanations of revolutions, wars, and so forth, in terms of personal or political prejudice, and one can find for such events as the French Revolution and the Napoleonic wars (see Geyl 1955) a wide range of conflicting and contradictory explanations. The Louis the Fat syndrome is not, of course, confined to historians, as the celebrated case of Redfield (1930) and Oscar Lewis (1951) in Tepoztlán may suggest, though here, since a restudy was involved, there is the possibility that the contradictory observations reflected changes that did take place.

One of the most important factors contributing to both observer and interpretational bias is ethnocentrism or lack of cultural relativism. For example, many, probably most, early observers of Afro-Asian peoples cast their descriptions in terms of their own cultural frameworks. In some cases this led to what might be called the "backward primitive" complex, the description of institutions in deprecatory terms, constantly emphasizing inferiority and difference vis-à-vis European models. Usually, on those occasions when institutions were favorably compared, it was in terms of their similarity to highly regarded idealized European institutions.

Two factors generally increased this observer bias: the physical and social distance of the observer from his observation and, in particular, lack of knowledge of local language and cultural context. Where these factors occur together, a highly biased account is most likely. Ethnocentrism and superficiality are particularly characteristic of many official papers in Afro-Asian archives. However, local linguistic and cultural knowledge, as the valuable mission sources show, can result in relatively unbiased sections, despite ulterior motives, since the approach, like that of modern anthropology, is from the inside.

Another factor likely to increase observer bias is what might be called expediency. Most observers live or work not only in a general cultural context but also within a specific institution. Within these institutions there are numerous demands and pressures for particular kinds of attitudes in reporting. The missionaries provide a good example of the effects of this kind of pressure. Especially in official reports, it was often expected that a missionary would write of the native religion in terms of its heathenism and to emphasize satanic and magical influences. Many missionaries in official reports also often exaggerated the virtues of converts and vices of nonconverts, who are portrayed as poor, inferior, and unhappy because of their beliefs. As we have noted, however, this institutional pressure did not stop the missionaries from writing relatively unbiased accounts when outside official focuses of interest or areas of control. Additionally, as in the case of spotting errors, observer bias may be due to such factors as particular quirks in the author's personality.

Interpretational bias is always present to some degree. In a recent paper Raymond W. Mack (M. Sherif and C. W. Sherif 1969:52) points out that the great majority of sociological investigation is colored by ethnocentrism and professional pressures and conventions. At some point the theoretical tools which the observer uses impart a bias to the research. In the documentary part of research work the selection of documents and methods of interpretation inevitably colors the ultimate analysis. Models, methods, and materials are inextricably intertwined, and the best the research worker can do is be aware of the bias, constantly adjusting theoretical approaches as new empirical material emerges.

Bias is also present when the observer records the facts himself. The observer cannot record everything he sees or hears. Even a camera records only one angle and a tape recorder one or a small number of proximate voices on a single theme. In any case these more complete recording devices yield too much data, and the bulk of fieldwork data must be selective notetaking. In this selection the observer must choose between different places and times, and then between different aspects of events. Most significant of all, during notetaking the form and functions of the notes reflect the observers own cultural and intellectual background, his prejudices and proclivities. This leads us to a very important point which has been generally overlooked in the literature. Because all records contain some kinds of bias, the differences between amateur and professional sources, or between the records of professionals of different disciplines, are differences of degree not kind. The techniques to be used in utilizing a historical source do not differ fundamentally from the techniques applied to the scrutiny of professional analyses. In all cases a thorough knowledge of the context of the document's authorship, and of the author's cultural and intellectual background, is the essential prerequisite for accurate interpretation.

However, this is not all that is needed. As I have said, the major procedures in dealing with bias are similar to the procedures involved in the establishment of the probability of facts. In fact, the higher the probability of facts, the lower the level of bias is likely to be. Important too is the author's own awareness of his bias. If this awareness is not present, or is misconstrued, then the research worker has the assessment to do. This requires more than knowledge of context. It necessitates a high degree of absorption in, or sympathy with, the historical observer. Barzun and Graff (1957:163) describe this process as one of triangulation, the points being the research worker (A), the historical observer (B), and the objects which he describes (C).

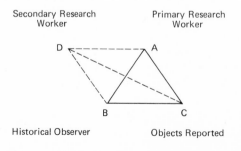

Secondary Research Worker   Primary Research Worker

D   A

B   C

Historical Observer   Objects Reported

All evaluations then are made through this triadic perspective, which minimizes the size of both research worker and observer bias. The use of triadic, tetradic, or higher order processes is especially important in analyzing secondary sources, that is, those which are not the product of the original observer. Some historians have felt that historical writing, and especially secondary reportage, is highly subjective, being intrinsically different among different authors, particularly if they lived in different times, places, or cultural contexts. We can clearly see that this is not the full story. In any triangle B and C remain constant, and even if it is not possible to bypass A—that is, to go back to the originals, D, B, C— then A is just one of three additional variables.

Semantics and Translation

There is one thing the research worker must be quite certain about in the process of establishing probabilities and accounting for bias. He must know, as far as is possible, the exact meaning of the words used in the document. Without this knowledge, the logical processes of internal criticism are quite inadequate. The basic task here is to know what the word means, not just in an absolute sense but relative to the semantic context in which it occurs. The research worker may assign from his own experience a given meaning or range of meanings to a particular word or word sequence. But these words or sequences have different meanings even in the same language at different times of history and in different dialects or idioms. Good examples are words like "democracy" or "property." Handlin (Handlin *et al.* 1966:24) has said that the history of the developing meaning of the word "corporation" is a history of American economic life. Meaning changes as well in different expression contexts. Some situations are more likely than others to produce meaning changes that occur in irony, satire, literary flourish, overstatement, and understatement. Nuance, inflection, and exaggeration are constantly present in all human documents.

These difficulties are increased when dealing, as many anthropologists do, with foreign language documents for which there are inadequate linguistic aids available. The problem is not so much that there will be preconceived ideas about verbal categories. Anthropologists learn many categories in a concrete fashion in the fieldwork situation. But a year or two in the field, even when combined with additional linguistic study, may not be enough to deal adequately with contextual meanings, especially in the analysis of highly allusive documents such as those dealing with myths.

The research worker also has to take great care in the historical observer's translation of foreign language words and concepts. For example, most of the early accounts of Afro-Asian peoples are filled with words and concepts derived from the European political, social, and economic structure. These may be very misleading. In Samoa, for instance, the French missionaries described the Samoan chiefs as "*seigneurs,*" analogous to the aristocracy of the *ancien régime.* Whereas, in fact, the chiefs' power was and is, in most cases, dependent on popular support and approval. In ensuring a high degree of semantic accuracy, there is once again no substitute for a detailed knowledge of the historical context. In addition, there should be a special study of the language, even if it is the research worker's own tongue.

Corroboration

The detection of errors, falsifications, biases, or distortions, and the like is a major historical method in establishing the probability of facts, or rather the compatability of the probable actuality and the statements about it. Equally important is verification, notably through the corroboration of evidence.

If many people record an event or feature in the same or similar ways, without collaboration, the degree of probability increases, but just how many witnesses constitute a critical mass is debatable. It may be difficult to establish the independence of witnesses, as they may be only repeating one another. Also, to a considerable extent, the existence of multiple recordings depends on the size of the documentary record. The anthropologist may be faced with a solitary record, especially in the early days of contact in many areas. If there is only one record there can be no corroboration, though there can be no contradiction either. Corroboration through alternative sources is more important in relatively recent times when there has been a multiplicity of institutions (and records) concerned with a single fact. For instance, newspaper records of recent events often help fill out official files.

The contemporary research worker also has means of corroborating evidence not usually utilized by historians, that is, through informants or through oral history and tradition. Informant history provides corroboration for several important kinds of documentary fact. Most significantly, great events (great political or religious occasions, rites of passage, natural disasters, periods of deprivation or personal distress) in the life of the society or person are remembered vividly and in detail.

The reliability of an informant's evidence is something the research worker comes to know as he comes to know the informant and his culture. Reliability is likely to increase as rapport with local society increases. But accuracy of evidence is affected by factors other than personal reliability. There are limits to personal memory. These constraints do not vary directly with time elapsed, though all things being equal, events of long ago are remembered less well than very recent events. Some people, however, have prodigious memories, and many can recall vividly a single or small number of details.

Important also are the kinds of material the informant is commenting on and his own personal position. For instance, if political information about contemporary situations is sought and the informant is himself involved in the process, then the information is likely to be confined in the same way as are official documents. Generally, these restrictions decline as one goes back in time, or as less-involved people are questioned. The actual situation of interviewing may be important too. For example, an informant is usually much more ready to disclose facts in a private discussion. There may be other tests which indicate reliability, such as internal consistency or consistency with probable facts in the written record. Even unreliable evidence may have its use since falsifications may deal with events or things which, because they are necessary to hide or distort, have some social significance.

Oral traditions differ from informant history in that they are testimonies which are formally transmitted from one generation to another, and in that they often have a specific form. Because they are remote from the original, on which they comment, because they are often literary rather than actual descriptions, oral traditions are perhaps of lesser value than informant history. However, they must be considered, if only because they may well provide the data on which later written accounts are based (for example, Southwold 1968). Moreover, as Jan Vansina (1965) has shown, it is possible to apply the tests of historical criticism to these traditions. In fact, oral traditions can provide valuable corroboration or extra evidence for certain aspects of the social structure. For example, data relating to religious facts are usually transmitted, because of their importance, with very great care and so are often accurate representations of past beliefs and practices. Historical accounts, whether in poetry or prose, often represent propaganda, for instance, the themes for Incan poetry laid down by the government, and are therefore useful in the study of past political attitudes. Lists of place names may be useful for demographic studies. The fact that oral traditions refer to situations prior to the period of documentary evidence is not necessarily a drawback, as the traditional society of the oral traditions usually extends well into the documentary period. In addition to oral traditions, further corroboration may be provided from archeological or linguistic evidence.

There is a danger, however, that the possibly factual oral traditions will be confused with marginally factual myth. So far the establishment of probability and accuracy has been considered in terms of a single frame of reference. Whatever intermediate tests or models we use, we are constantly evaluating against a background of what is, in many ways, no more than common sense. We accept, reject, select, and sort according to known or assumed propensities and characteristics of human behavior, that is, in a context of a frame of what we conceive to be reality. But this is not the only possible frame of reference. Recently, for instance, Levi-Strauss (1970), following the lead of Durkheim, has argued that myth is an alternative frame of reference with a logic of its own. Myths in this sense do not explain or reflect any feature of the social structure. They are, Levi-Strauss says, analogous to musical systems, languages in their own right.

The techniques for studying myth have relevance for our interest in historical criticism. Anthropologists particularly have to deal with recorded myths that describe possible events. It becomes necessary then to recognize when an account is mythical. This may be a simple task if the myth contains impossible or extremely unlikely events (such as men living forever, or humans existing in animal form), but all myths contain some probable and possible facts. Moreover, it is possible that all historical accounts contain mythical elements. Levi-Strauss (1970:12–13) implies that this is why there are different and contradictory descriptions of the same event (for example, the French Revolution).

Critical methods, particularly corroboration, can get around some of these problems. More significantly, myth (like music) occurs usually as a complex inter-related arrangement of units and not as a single unit within an historical account. Myths then, even when concerned with historical or possible events, can often be recognized by their general shape, and perhaps by other features such as their anaclasticism (Levi-Strauss 1970:5).

Despite the chances of corroboration, there will always remain a large body of unverified evidence, of possible facts. The assessment of probability may be assisted by circumstantial evidence, by how well one fact fits in with others of greater probability. Interpretational as well as circumstantial evidence is also important. A great many historical facts owe their credibility, as Professor Carr has pointed out (1964:12), to the fact that they fit in with this or that theory or thesis. However, it is important for the research worker to try and use other validity tests before this one.

Coverage Deficiencies

Another very important difference between documentary and field work or survey data relates to the coverage of reporting. On the one hand; in the fieldwork situation or in a survey, the data recorded is, to a considerable extent, the field-worker's choice. Certainly, there may be subjects, places, or times which are temporarily restricted, but at least the fieldworker has a definite schedule of information he wants. On the other hand, the documentary record represents other peoples' choices of data to be recorded and preserved.

Inevitably, the historical record, vis-à-vis the fieldwork or survey record, contains certain gaps and deficiencies. These gaps are of several kinds. First, there are the gaps imposed in the public archives on the time availability of documents or their confidentiality. Second, there are the gaps created by the accidental or deliberate destruction of papers. This is especially a problem in local archives, where records are simply not kept or are periodically weeded. Third, there are the gaps created by the research worker himself through his unconscious or conscious selection of documents to be looked at or facts to be recorded. Fourth, there are the gaps created by the selectivity of the reporters.

The reportage of any event is recorded in a qualitatively different way by anthropologists or sociologists, on the one hand, and by officials, missionaries, and such, on the other hand. Officials' notes are not destined to become learned monographs but are utilized for specific reports. Seldom will the reporter either indulge in recording inconsequential details or allow his imagination to explore possible explanations of an event, a characteristic of many anthropological field-work notebooks. Many times in the record, in fact, an observer will stop short, or describe a highly significant event in agonizingly generalized terms. This generality is particularly unfortunate in two important respects. Personal and place names may be omitted from the historical record far more often than they would be in fieldwork reporting. Certainly, persons in high political offices may be named, though there is a tendency to use general descriptive terms—chief, leader, prince, and so forth. Generality is much more marked as one descends the social scale, or as one moves outside the focuses of political power.

In addition, there are subject concentrations stemming from bias or job considerations—for example, administration records focus on political activities, and mission records on processes of religious change. Other deficiencies may result because reporters have inadequate knowledge of the local language or customs.

As a consequence of all this, subjects of great interest recorded and detailed in the field are inadequately covered in the historical record. One good example is kinship data; another is material on personality. Both these fields have been neglected by historians, not in the least because of lack of documentary evidence. On the other hand, recent work by Eric Erikson (1959) and Alain Besançon (1967) have shown the possibilities of psychoanalytical history using letters and literature.

The quantitative historical record is in some ways less deficient in certain respect vis-à-vis the field record than the qualitative record. This is partly because in many official organizations the collection of statistics is, or was, an important function. Possibly, it is also a result of the fact that anthropologists have used relatively simple quantitative fieldwork techniques and have fewer expectancies in this respect. There has been a certain suspicion about statistics (especially by British social anthropologists), and very detailed statistical coverage, even for a small unit, is a great time- and resource-consuming task.

Nevertheless, there are important gaps and deficiencies in the quantitative historical record. Censuses have only been conducted at long intervals in many parts of Afro-Asia, using different enumeration techniques and areas at different times and thus making analysis very difficult. The unreliability of such statistics may also be considerable. Often all that remains are the bare figures for a territory or district in a year, the detailed returns on which these returns were based having been destroyed or lost. Once again, statistics are usually only available insofar as they have a use in the political apparatus, and the categories are those which are officially understood, approved, or recognized. Hence important frequencies (for example, illegal marital forms or important class or traditional distinctions) may not be recorded.

To some extent the problems arising from faulty coverage can be ameliorated in much the same way as corroboration is achieved. Informant history particularly may be used to plug certain gaps or provide extra material. Informants may be not only people from the local society but also persons involved in the administration or mission machinery. Retired people, especially, freed from organizational pressures, may well be prepared to provide valuable information. Fortunately, also, when there is a multiple recording of events, the gaps in one record may not be replicated in another. For example, some material from confidential documents is often contained in open files. Local archives have usually less stringent rules on time limits. Newspaper files are again very useful for the contemporary period.

Generality may be more difficult to counter. But the anonymity of the local area or special group can sometimes be penetrated through special records. For example, historian George Rudé (1958) has been able to examine in detail (through the skillful use of police records) the social characteristics of the "crowd," the lower classes who participated in some of the violent events of the

French Revolution. This kind of record, especially in periods of stress or strain (rebellions, revolutions, riots, depressions, and so forth), can be of critical importance since great detail is present, and since at such times important aspects of the social structure are dramatically revealed. Unfortunately, these documents often have a short life expectancy or are kept in the most confidential places.

Inference

Historians have also used another method to get around some of the problems raised by gaps and deficiencies in the record, that is, inference, or extended interpretation. Through inferential methods relationships between, or the consequences of, known facts or events can be assessed. Quite often in historical studies a relationship is assumed if there is a coincidence in time between two events.

There are a number of real problems in inferential explanations. First, because two events occur coincidentally, there is not necessarily any relevant connection between them; they might well have their own separate explanations. Very often the historian, in inferring connections of this kind, or in postulating a likely concomitant of an event or fact, is drawing on analogies in other regions, or models involving similar kinds of facts. Second, there is the "chicken and egg" problem; if two events occur simultaneously and are related, which way does the causal relationship run, or does it run both ways, as the functionalists would have it. Third, there is what has been called the problem of the false dilemma (Kitson Clark 1967:57). If only a small number of factors are reported for a given situation, then a choice of any other factor is much less certain or even impossible. It is difficult to resist using a known piece of evidence when there is little idea of the other factors at work.

Similar problems arising from the incompleteness in the historical record occur also in fieldwork, but not to the same extent. If an anthropologist has doubts about a certain kind of relationship, he can test hypotheses by asking people or by observation. Documents cannot be interviewed, but the good historical research worker will follow up leads by looking for evidence in perhaps unlikely places. Even if in the first report only one or two factors are mentioned, a range of possible contributory factors may be hypothecated at work in any similar situation, and a search can be started in the appropriate records for possible verification. In any case the historian cannot usually cover the whole of the written record relevant to his subject.

Inference is helped by the semantic understanding which has just been described. The primary purpose is not to know just what the documents formally say but rather what the author intended to say, and to interpret any behavior described in its own context. Inference, then, as in the case of assessing subjectivity or semantic and behavioral meaning, involves cultural and temporal relativism.

What this means is that the research worker must steep himself in the literature of the period and culture from which his important authors originate.

If, for example, we are utilizing mission sources, we should read, in addition to the basic documents, the autobiographies of the missionaries, general histories, the literature of the period, and mission histories, as well as dip into the relevant theological books, and probably talk to modern-day missionaries of the same order. The great French social historian Bloch, who has written the definitive history of the medieval French countryside (1966), used to travel widely through the French villages of his day, discussing his problems not only with local savants but also with the everyday bucolic countryman. Through this kind of absorption, the research worker is able to develop a touch and empathy which allows keener interpretation and perception.

Inferential methods have also been used by historians to discover hidden, extended, oblique, or allegorical meanings in texts or reports (hermeneutics, exegesis, and so forth). Such works, apart from mythological or religious documents, will probably have a limited utility in anthropological documentary research.

Another kind of extended interpretation used by historians is what is usually called "content analysis" (North *et al.* 1963, Berelson 1952). In this method it is postulated that the frequency of occurrence in a text of a word, theme, character, concept, or item (Berelson 1952:135) can be correlated with a given social fact. Content analysis lends itself to quantification and has been used particularly in political studies, but potentially, content analysis can be used in a wide variety of problems. A good example of the sophisticated use of this technique is a recent study of family patterns in eighteenth-century America (Lantz *et al.* 1968). In this study Lantz and his colleagues used fifteen magazines (comprising 546 issues) which were published in New England in the period 1741–1794. Their main object was to provide data on key features of the American family such as the romantic love complex and marital motives, freedom of mate choice, husband–wife and parent–child relations, and sexual standards in the preindustrial period. In discussing "romantic love," the authors first picked out the number of times romantic love is discussed in the magazine articles as the motive for marriage vis-à-vis other motives, such as wealth or status. They find that romantic love far outweighs the other motives and conclude, contrary to many traditional views, that notions of romantic love preceded industrialization.

Gaps in statistical information pose special problems. However, there are inferential mathematical techniques (for example, multivariate analysis) for providing estimates to fill certain gaps resulting from incomplete time or spatial coverage. The relative validity of these estimates is ultimately dependent on the volume of the data, and in many cases in Afro-Asia, particularly, there simply are not enough data. Frequently, for example, there are general historical statistics which are not, however, broken down for the geographical or subject areas in which the research worker is interested. In these cases it may be possible to provide some kind of local estimate, if the relationship between the local and general statistics is known at more than one point in time, and if there have been no dramatic changes in the local area or in its relationship with other areas. If, let us say, per capita income or output in our village are approximately $x\%$ below the national mean during the fieldwork period, and if there are no reports of dramatic changes in the village economy during the previous periods, then it is probable that village wealth has remained of this order. In this case, it may be possible to extrapolate local figures from national figures for earlier periods.

The analysis of demographic changes almost always requires a good deal of statistical inference. Census information, at best, is usually taken at ten-year intervals, and in early periods of contact even simple estimates of numbers may be hundreds of years apart. Even if we leave aside the knotty problems of differential reliability of sources, and even if we work in a period where census material is available at ten-year periods, the assumption is often made that the demographic characteristics at any point in time vary directly in relation to the characteristics at the census dates. Where there is reliable and frequent evidence, this is probably a reasonable assumption, but such inferences may be meaningless, especially in early periods.

Sequences, Patterns, and Causes

Evaluation and interpretation can only proceed so far by assessing the validity of facts. A stage is reached when the individual pieces have to be placed together. The simplest conjunction is the chronological, that is, putting a date on documents or facts reported in the documents and arranging them in that order. Dating itself may be a complicated business. Some documents are undated, and estimates must be made from the position of a document in a collection (provided the collection has not been disturbed), or from internal indications, such as the dates of people who feature in the documents or the events described. Even when documents are dated, there are complications such as the transfer from the Julian to the Gregorian calendar, which took place in different countries at different times, or different names of months or styles of dating.

Chronological order, however, does not necessarily imply that there is any further link between the events or situations described. The next and perhaps the most important concern of all is to try to establish patterns of causality (that is, links of cause and effect between two facts or events), or other kinds of conjunction and classification. Causal analysis will form a major part of the process of analysis in the writing up once the documentary evidence has been sifted and is therefore outside the scope of this discussion. Even when collecting and sorting documents, however, some idea of the causal framework has to be appreciated. The research worker has to be aware of a range of possibilities about which historians and philosophers have debated at great length.

The search for causes is an ancient commonplace in historical research. Herodotus, to many the father of modern history, defined his purpose in writing as to preserve the memory of both the Greeks and the Barbarians, and, more fundamentally, to show causes—why they fought each other. This search for causes remains today in all schools of history. All historians seek to weigh and establish priorities for causal patterns. Some work in a context of multiple causes. Others, although dealing with multiplicities, search for critical causes in the hierarchy, the cause of other, or all, causes. In its extreme form there are historical models (for example, models derived from Marx, Spengler, or Freud) in which it is postulated that the causes of any event follow a well-defined and established pattern from a single major origin, that there is an inevitability of certain events following certain causes.

To be contrasted with these kinds of theories of historical determinism are theories, such as those of Popper (1957) and Berlin (1955), in which chance, accident, or human free will play the major role in causality. To some extent this school of history has developed what has been called the "Cleopatra nose" characteristic (Carr 1964:19). This is the characteristic of explaining a large-scale event by a chance accident or minor event, in this case Antony losing the battle of Actium because of his infatuation with Cleopatra. At its extreme there are historians who follow the existentialist philosophers in saying that there are no causes for events and therefore little need for causal classification. There are also many historians (see, for example, Barzun and Graff 1957:150ff), who regard the search for causes, especially critical causes, to be of no great importance since each event and situation is regarded as unique. For these pragmatic historians, as Barzun calls them, it is enough to see the background and antecedents.

Of course, in some measure these concerns about the nature of causation have been common to all the social sciences and have been reflected in the sociological and anthropological literature (for example, MacIver 1942), though the focus has been rather on simultaneous and continuing relationships such as those derived from functionalist theory.

There remain two other classification problems which affect the research process at an early stage. First, how should facts be grouped in the time dimension? Historians often look at their evidence in the context of a given period. The period under study is usually lengthy, centuries or longer (though there have been exceptions, as in the work of Sir Lewis Namier) or with definite times which are considered to be qualitatively different from their predecessors and successors (for example, the ancient, medieval, and modern periods). Within the shorter kind of period there is often an assumption of structural homogeneity, but there is a tendency to deal with the facts in a chronological context. A favorite device of historians is to look for what is often called the "watershed," the point in time at which new sets of social or usually political facts came into being. In contrast, the anthropologist's or sociologist's time is usually structural rather than chronological. His facts are not so much events as social relationships, and any sequences are measured in terms of these relationships. For instance, an anthropologist looking at a kinship sequence will not usually talk about years but about rites of passage, the development cycle, and structural arrangements, often grouping together facts which are temporally dispersed.

Second, there is the problem of knowing how far back to go in the record. The studies of most anthropologists and sociologists are anchored in the present and the question is: How far does this period extend back in time? In many cases in Afro-Asia this is not a real problem, for the historical documents only refer to a given, short time period. But in Europe or America there may be a very long historical record. For example, for villages in the Canton of Vaud in Switzerland there may be records stretching back to Roman times, and certainly there are village records from the tenth or eleventh century on. The question of how relevant these kinds of records may be varies greatly with the kind of record remaining, and also the fieldwork problem. If, for example, the anthropologist is studying a modern village, data from the contemporary period rather from the medieval or classical world will be relevant, and there will be a steeply diminishing rate of return in the earlier periods. But these periods may still contain useful information on societal features, such as kinship, which may not have changed as drastically as the polity or the economy.

Specifically, the methods to be used in establishing patterns of causality or classification represent the culmination of the processes of external and internal criticism of documentary evidence. Wherever the research worker stands on the causality issue, the jobs of weighing the likelihood of this or that relationship has to be done. As in all other stages of historical analysis, the researcher should keep an open mind, though he has to be aware of the range of models for interpretation.

Further Reading

There are a large number of guides to the critical handling of documentary evidence. The most useful guides are the classic work of the French historiographers Langlois and Seignobos (1898), Bloch's (1954) brilliant, unfinished fragment, written by the great French social historian while he fought in the Resistance during the World War II, and Gottschalk's *Understanding History*. (1969). Other useful guides are those by Barzun and Graff (1957), Hockett (1955), Garraghan and Delanglez (1946), and Kent (1954). Older but still useful are the works by Vincent (1911) and George (1909). Useful, if more general, comments have been made by Carr (1964), Kitson Clark (1967), and Nevins (1962), and are included as well in the Social Science Research Council studies mentioned in Chapter 2. Handlin (Handlin *et al.* 1966:25) provides a list of papers on modern techniques of external criticism.

There is an interesting section on bias in the book by Barzun and Graff (1957:159ff), and the student should also read Mack's essay on bias (M. Sherif and C. W. Sherif 1969). The literature on translation is restricted (see Postgate 1922), but Gudschinsky (1967) provides details of the ways in which the cultural anthropologist handles an unwritten language.

The literature on interpretation is vast. Meyerhoff (1959) and Stern (1956) have compiled useful anthologies. Barnes (1961) has written a brief review. Walsh (1951) has written a good introduction to the philosophy of history, and the student should read the book by Geyl (1955). Gottschalk (1969: 221ff) provides an excellent section on causality, while Handlin (Handlin *et al.* 1966:15ff) provide a useful summary and bibliography. An interesting way of getting an insight into the changing currents of historical philosophies is to read the presidential addresses to the American Historical Association in the *American Historical Review* (for example, Morison 1951, Bridenbaugh 1963). Finally, for a lighthearted but perceptive introduction to the philosophy of history through vignettes of leading European scholars, the book by Mehta (1963) is recommended.

5

A Case Study: Social Context and Economic Development in Samoa

S O FAR I have dealt mainly with general points concerning the utility of historical documents. A specific example which illustrates some of the possibilities of historical analysis and also some of the pitfalls, difficulties, and dangers will now be considered. This case study may also indicate how the next and most difficult process, that of analysis and exposition, can be begun.

Models and Problems

One of the most famous debates common to history and the social sciences has ranged around the question of the social context of economic activity. In cultural anthropology (see, for example, Cook 1966) the argument has revolved around the question of whether or not the maximization theories of the classical economists are really applicable to traditional societies. On the one hand, anthropologists, beginning notably with Raymond Firth (1929), claimed a good deal of applicability, while on the other hand, the followers of Karl Polanyi, the so-called substantivists (see, for example, Dalton 1966), painted a picture of an altruistic economy based on prestige and status, different in kind from the European capitalist economies.

These distinctions between different kinds of economies were apparent also in the writings of sociologists and economic historians in the nineteenth century, especially those influenced by the Hegelian dialectic. But in the twentieth century the debate crystallized around a particular aspect of the problem, the assertion by Max Weber (1930) that the essential correlate of capitalist development was a particular social context best exemplified by the Protestant religion. The Protestant context emphasized and rewarded the individual pursuit of worldly ends, rationality, innovativeness, and acquisition.

Historians [see, for example, Green (1959)] were most concerned with the validity of Weber's model for Reformation Europe, but more recently, sociologists [such as S. N. Eisenstadt (1968)] and economists [like W. A. Lewis (1955)] have taken up the basic idea to help explain modernization and the plight of the underdeveloped nations of the world. Here, too, the ideas of the substantivist and like-minded anthropologists were utilized, and what emerged was a model in which the traditional institutions of Afro-Asian societies, the antithesis of Weber's ideal type, were seen as a—perhaps *the*—fundamental obstacle to economic development (that is, rises in per capita consumption or production).

My object was to examine the validity of this model through a detailed case study of a particular society, the Western Samoan Islands in the South Pacific (Pitt 1970). I chose Samoa because of long residence in the Pacific and some familiarity with the Islands rather than for any heuristic reason, though I was to discover later that the social structure presented evidence both interesting and extremely pertinent to my argument.

Although I intended to gather much data from fieldwork, that is, from direct and intensive observation on the spot, it was clear at the outset that a great deal of historical research was needed and desirable. After all the basic question was one of process, the relationship of one kind of development (social) to another (economic) involving fundamentally the history of culture contact.

Methods

The first major problem was methodological, involving particularly the location of available documents. Although there are excellent bibliographies of printed materials relating to Samoa (Taylor 1965), there are only general indications as to where one might find manuscript sources. First of all, letters were written, or visits were paid, to the major European institutions concerned with Samoa. Consultation of these documents created a logistical difficulty, for these institutions were spread across the world. Many of the missions had their headquarters in Europe, but the bulk of the official and administration papers were located in the United States and New Zealand, and there were other important collections in Australia and Hawaii. Not all these documents could be consulted after the fieldwork, and it was difficult to know initially what specific information to extract. Especially in the mission houses, there were mountains of papers concerned with even such a small island group. Certainly, there were obvious, general culture-contact materials concerned with relevant topics such as the spread of cash cropping, wage labor, trading, and social structure. At this stage, however, it was difficult to integrate historical and fieldwork research. For one thing, I did not know before going to Samoa which villages or districts I would be working in and could not, therefore, take detailed notes on particular areas. Fortunately, perhaps, many of the European documents were either generalized for the whole group or referred to the main town of Apia and its environs. Also, of course, even if one could not revisit the far-flung documentary sources, relevant material could be photocopied at a later date.

In Samoa itself the location and use of documents was in one sense easier since most were located in the institutions in the main town and consultation could easily be fitted in with fieldwork. However, archives were seldom organized, there were no facilities for photocopying, and a great many documents were lost, destroyed, or eaten beyond recognition by the ubiquitous tropical paperbugs and rats.

Although long and arduous, the task of recording relevant data did not pose any special problems. Much greater difficulties arose in utilizing data in the discussion of my major theoretical concern, the role of traditional institutions in economic development.

External Impetus

Economic development in Samoa can be conceptualized as being dependent on two not always distinct kinds of process. On the one hand, there is the external impetus coming from European capital, commerical, colonial, and mission activity. On the other hand, there is the internal generation of development through the demands and organizational changes in the local society. This distinction emphasizes the important point that economic development is often a problem of culture contact or stratification rather than a problem of the relationships between two kinds of institutions.

I was struck during my stay in Samoa with the social separation between people who called themselves Europeans and people who called themselves Samoans (in both groups many were of mixed descent). The Europeans lived generally in the main town of Apia, while most Samoans lived in rural villages or in separate suburbs in Apia. Even those Europeans (for example, the missionaries, the planters) who were out in the countryside lived apart from the villages.

From the historical records the origins and dynamics of this separation became quite clear. Early mission and trader's documents showed that initially the Europeans had been dependent on the Samoan villages for food and protection, and there had been a good deal of integration and direct assistance by the Europeans in local economic development, in introducing, for example, the important export of copra. After the foundation of the town of Apia, however, the Europeans drifted away from the villages, and the new Europeans did not venture outside the town boundary. Two minimally related sectors were created in the Samoan economy. Throughout the twentieth century, the administration records, particularly, show how little assistance was given to village development.

At this stage there were some problems of critical analysis in handling the documentary evidence. For example, the evidence on the very early settlers in the villages is scanty. These men were castaways, shipwrecked, abandoned by their ships because of disease, even desperate convicts from the New South Wales penal settlement. Few recorded any details of their lives. Most accounts come from the early missionaries, who often portray the beachcombers in horrific colors, blaming them for introducing liquor, syphilis, war, and so forth, and generally disrupting village life. But there may be reasons for distrusting some of the mission testimony. The missions had little contact with the castaways and were in a sense in competition with them since many castaways set themselves up as resident priests. There is contrary evidence too from other, later, reputable mission observers. The circumstantial evidence also contradicts the horror tales. The castaways, until the arrival of regular shipping services in the 1840s, had no access to liquor or arms, and the first authenticated cases of syphilis do not occur until 1848—suspiciously close to the time of a visit by one of Her Majesty's warships. Evidence preserved in trading company archives suggests that both the castaways and early traders did much to help village development.

Internal Generation

At least since the mid-nineteenth century, the Europeans did little to help local development. Conversely, one might expect that the development which did occur was the product of local initiatives and endeavors. Most of my study was concerned with the problem of finding evidence to indicate how far local institutions had in fact contributed to economic progress.

First, the broad pattern of village economic participation had to be established. Once again there were many documentary gaps, particularly in the nineteenth century, but local records collected by the various administrations[1] showed that in the twentieth century most villages had participated actively in cash cropping and wage labor. Certainly, this could not be an absolute quantitative measure since many figures were unreliable by the standards of present-day statistical services. But other evidence helped construct the picture. At this stage I had chosen the fieldwork villages and had conducted a fieldwork survey of the present production patterns. This provided a check on contemporary records. From administration records and discussions with villagers, I gained some idea of vital factors in the production process, such as the labor force or land use, all of which helped to establish an approximate idea of village efforts.

Values

The next problem was to establish the societal concomitants of this development. An important part of the Weberian explanation is the emphasis on the values of a society in promoting development, particularly those values which support the acquisition of useful or potentially productive goods, hard work, and careful, thrifty expenditure. This involved an analysis of attitudes, on the one hand, and key behavioral indicators (for example, consumption patterns and expenditure and time budgets), on the other.

In investigating attitudes, the insufficiency of locally originating material was immediately obvious, for there were very few historical records of attitudes to

---

[1] The Europeans established a bicameral legislature of chiefs in 1873. The Germans were awarded Western Samoa as part of a great power agreement in 1900. The British occupied Western Samoa in 1914, and after this New Zealand administered the territory, first, as a League of Nations mandate, and later, starting in 1945, as a United Nations Trust Territory. Independence was achieved in 1962.

goods, wealth, and work. One possible source of evidence is the proverbs which are an important part of Samoan speech and the oral literature, widely used in reference to economic activity. References may be highly allusive and metaphorical. One example is the proverb *O le Malie ma le tu'u malie*. Literally, this proverb is translated "For the shark there is the shark gift." When a fisherman catches a shark, he must present the village with the first (and possibly the only) shark, though he does receive other gifts. The meaning is that for every action there is a reaction or retribution. In economic activity everything has a price. Other proverbs have a more direct reference. For example, there is a proverb *Fa le taeao e le afiafi*—the man who sleeps in the morning will not eat in the evening (the time of the principal meal). This proverb emphasizes the need for hard work and consideration of future needs if life is to be enjoyed.

Many proverbs have been collected by the missionaries and by ethnographically minded administrators. But usually in this record there is only a scanty note on proverb usage, especially the wide-ranging metaphorical meanings. Most proverbs relevant to economic activity were either obtained from fieldwork or checked out in context with contemporary informants.

The documentation on behavioral indicators is much firmer. For example, a good time depth and considerable detail can be acquired for income and the consumption of European goods. Early consular records record the amounts and kinds of goods moving in and out of the islands as part of the commercial information relayed to home governments. Most goods moved through the main port of Apia, and the consuls had a good knowledge of trade since they themselves were deeply involved in it. When European-style governments were established, the monitoring of imports and exports became very detailed, for a great deal of official revenue was derived from tariffs and levies.

From this historical evidence it could be shown that there had been an expanding demand for goods, especially utilitarian and capital goods. However, most of the evidence was generalized for the whole territory, and there were only scraps of information to be found for specific villages, usually from traders' records, when these existed or access was permitted. Similarly, only scanty historical data could be found from which to construct time budgets, though there existed both qualitative evidence from traditional material (proverbs and legends again) and government files indicating a relatively high level of work performance.

Property

Another important feature of all societal explanations of economic development is the role of institutions in allowing individuals rights to the rewards for their economic efforts. Underdevelopment has generally been correlated with a relatively low level of rights in goods and services and consequent low incentives. Put simply, if a man cannot see some tangible fruits for his labor, he will not work hard.

The task in Samoa was to examine the distribution of rights and their relationship to economic activity. It was necessary at the outset to distinguish between two interrelated kinds of rewards. On the one hand, there are material returns in goods or services, and, on the other hand, there are rewards in status, in prestige, in position within the social structure.

The first set of questions concerned property rights. To what extent was private property part of the traditional Samoan social structure? This question necessitated an examination of a wide range of village goods, particularly land, which has played such an important part in agricultural development.

Much of the fieldwork evidence indicated that there existed in the contemporary village a wide range of goods over which an individual had very extensive rights of use, consumption, and disposal. Had this been true in the past? The historical record was not particularly useful in regard to personal goods, though there were some important insights. One feature of personal property in Samoa is its close actual or symbolic connection with the person; personal goods are either worn, in close contact with the body (for example, sleeping equipment), or kept in private places—for example, under mats or in locked boxes or trunks. This proximity not only allows control over the goods but tends as well to imbue the goods with the kind of *tapu* which surrounds the body. That this feature of ownership goes well back into Samoan history can be demonstrated from the early mission and exploration records. For example, Captain Wilkes (1847 vol. 2:78) describes vividly how one woman tried to wear all her personal possessions, going to church swaddled in yards of calico. The missionaries frequently remark on the trunks and boxes, and these can be clearly seen in photographs of the interiors of Samoan houses taken by German colonists.

However, the discussion of land tenure was quite a different proposition. Land has been such an important element in the history of culture contact in Samoa, a source of so much argument and litigation, that there is a massive and very detailed archive remaining. In the nineteenth century an international commission was established to arbitrate on European claims to land; more significantly, however, in the twentieth century a court (the Land and Titles Court) was set up to provide an arena for arguments about traditional rights in land and chiefly titles. During its history every family in Samoa and virtually every piece of land has been before the court. The court records contain not only specific details on boundaries but a mass of data on the traditional rules of tenure.

In this sphere historical research led the fieldwork in unraveling the evidence. Land tenure was not an easy subject to discuss in the village. Boundaries and rights were, for many people, secret matters. Only one village in Samoa had been surveyed, and this had led to a rebellion.

From the court records, particularly, there emerged a picture of different kinds of rights over different kinds of land. Over the house and its small surrounding section there existed a tenure very similar to European freehold. In the forest and the lagoons, land was held in common by the village, and any man from the village had the right of use. Most important economically, gardenland, the land on which the export crops (copra, cacao, bananas) were grown, was "owned," in a sense, by the *'āiga* (broadly, the communal extended family).

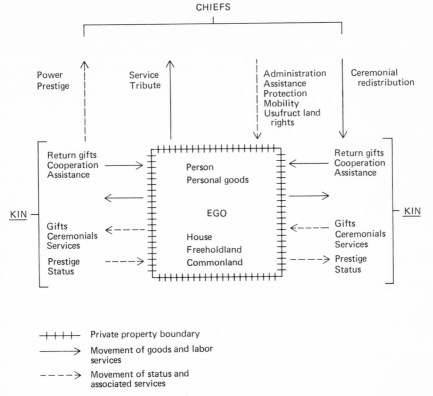

CHIEFS

Power
Prestige

Service
Tribute

Administration
Assistance
Protection
Mobility
Usufruct land
rights

Ceremonial
redistribution

Return gifts
Cooperation
Assistance

Person
Personal goods

Return gifts
Cooperation
Assistance

KIN

EGO

KIN

Gifts
Ceremonials
Services

House
Freeholdland
Commonland

Gifts
Ceremonials
Services

Prestige
Status

Prestige
Status

┼┼┼┼┼ Private property boundary

──────> Movement of goods and labor
services

─ ─ ─ ─> Movement of status and
associated services

Even here, however, the individual had extensive rights of usufruct, rights to the reward for any input of labor.

Chiefs and Community

Individual rights in goods and services are only one side of the coin. They exist relative to other kinds of pressures on these resources forcing the individual to disburse his property. In Samoa demands on goods and services come from two directions in the social structure, vertically, from the chiefs, and horizontally, from kin (*'āiga*) (see diagram). Those who claim that the traditional social structure is an obstacle to development in Samoa (or in Afro-Asia generally) see these hierarchical and communal demands as depriving the individual of any accumulated wealth and, hence, of any incentive to steady, let alone increased, economic effect.

Once again the fieldwork evidence pointed to limits on the extent of and occasions on which these chiefly and kin demands could be made. There were also clearly returns in goods, services, or status for any outgoing goods and services (see diagram). Once again the historical evidence bolstered this finding. There were mission and administration records concerned with the power of the chiefs, for both missionary and administrator were concerned with the extent to which the chief would be the agent of European influence, or subservient to European wishes. The pattern of government and conversion in Samoa was indirect. It had to be. The number of resident Europeans were too small to influence more than a handful of villagers, and in any case the European gentlemen preferred to live in the comfort of the port town of Apia.

Particularly useful when looking at evidence on the power of the chiefs were the government papers (including a Royal Commission) on the *Mau* (resistance) rebellions. There were two important *Mau* (one each during the German and New Zealand administrations) when a coterie of chiefs attempted to thwart the colonial hegemony. The documentation surrounding constitutional evolution was almost as important as the revolutionary material. Before independence (1962) there was a commission on local government which visited and heard and recorded detailed evidence in almost every village in the islands. There was much evidence too in the papers of the constitutional conferences which met immediately prior to independence, and at which an attempt was made to retain much of the traditional structure in the new state. Again the Land and Titles Court records contain much interesting information. The Court was concerned not just with the chief's authority in land matters but also with the whole question of *tautua* (service). *Tautua* includes all the labor an individual must contribute to his kin group (*'āiga*) and to his village as part of the duties involved in residence. The chief could not be a despot. An individual had the right of appeal to village or district councils (*fono*) and eventually to the Court itself. This procedure most chiefs disliked since it carried with it the disgraceful implication that the chief was a cruel man. More specifically, relationships between chiefs and commoners, like relations between kin, were reciprocal. The chief depended on goods and support from below to redistribute and use in prestige-giving ceremonial disbursement. There was a small amount of evidence in the Court files and traders' records on tribute and gift giving, though this aspect generally had to be investigated in the field.

Status and Mobility

Status reward was also a problem for which historical data was very illuminating. The most important status in Samoan society is that of the chief (*matai*). These titles are also ranked and graded both within the village and, at least for the higher titles, on a national basis. It was first necessary to find out the rules of succession, for, in general, the critics of traditional institutions (see, for example, Smelser and Lipset 1966) had blamed ascriptive status and limited mobility for development defects.

The details of succession are in the form of a genealogical historical record (*gafa*), though this has been preserved orally, handed down from one *tulafale* (orator chief, traditional custodian of *gafa*) to the next. However, *gafa*—especially for important families—have been recorded at various times since the mid-nineteenth century by missionaries, amateur and professional ethnographers, administrators, and the like. Most of these *gafa* show a high degree of ascription, especially in earlier generations, but careful comparison shows anomalies in recent times. Fieldwork bore out the hypothesis that ascription (for example, primogeniture) is built into the genealogy, whatever the real relationship, and in some cases there was no biological relationship.

There was a similar situation with regard to the ranking of titles. This ranking is recorded for each village in the formal address of welcome (fa'alupega). Again, the Europeans have recorded at different times the fa'alupega, and again there are changes in the relative rankings. This happened even when the published fa'alupega froze the actual structure. In the early part of the twentieth century the London Missionary Society, the largest of the missions, collected and published all the fa'alupega. But ways were found of circumventing this list. For example, in one fieldwork village the titles called out in the speech of welcome were, in fact, not single titles but groups of titles. Historical records (of chiefs who signed letters or petitions to the government, for example) showed that this group was constantly changing, reflecting the currents of power and prestige.

The essential link between mobility and economic ability was more difficult to demonstrate historically. There were registers of chiefs going back to the beginning of the German period (1900), initially for poll tax assessment and later for electoral purposes. From these, some idea of the dynamics of titleholding emerged. The first significant fact was that there was a relatively constant ratio (6–9%) between the number of titles and the actual population. Old titles were split as many as twenty times, and new titles were created, with some titleholders holding as many as four titles. It was quite clear that the structure was very flexible and that the majority of Samoans, including women, had the opportunity of obtaining a title. The Land and Titles Court files contained further evidence that economic and leadership aptitudes were what counted in rival claims for titles and not birth or any other ascribed characteristics.

From both fieldwork and historical data it could be seen that important incentives toward economic activity were provided in the reward system of Samoan society. In fact, one could go further and argue that the communal groups, the 'āiga and village groups, with their chiefs, were important and essential organizations in the general absence of successful European institutions. The communal groups could provide a base for cooperative work activity, elementary social security services, mutual assistance in all production activities, and credit and capital formation. The chiefs could provide leadership, middleman, and managerial skills.

Historical examples of successful organizations were to be found. There were, for instance, the papers relating to cooperative and community development movements. Even when these experiments were failures, the cause of failure could often be detected outside the village, usually in the shortcomings of an ethnocentric European bureaucracy.

Capital and Entrepreneurship

The critics of the traditional system have also picked on two other major societal obstacles to economic development in countries such as Samoa—the absence of capital formation and entrepreneurial activity. Once again documentary evidence was very useful in arguing against this proposition. Traditional technology had been recorded in great detail by the early ethnographers, and there was extensive evidence on the introduction of modern technology, especially in the administration agricultural files. The development of money, savings, and investment could be carefully plotted and documented from the records of the savings banks, credit unions, cooperative societies, and so forth. There was, similarly, much on human capital (that is, health and education) in the relevant government files. Information on trading and other entrepreneurial activity could be obtained from trading and business house archives, cooperative records, and government files (for example, Inland Revenue). From these records, as much as from fieldwork, a pattern emerged of steady Samoan involvement and progress in capital activities.

Most interesting of all, these capital and entrepreneurial activities were carried on within the traditional structure of Samoan society. Loans were raised and business was carried on through the support of the 'āiga, the relatives. Business could not exist without the relatives, for European interests would not support those enterprises they considered to be bad risks.

Labor

So far most of the analysis has concerned economic activities in the village, but another very important socioeconomic phenomenon was the movement of village labor to the towns and abroad, mainly in search of work and wealth. There have been many social scientists who have argued that such movement contributes as much as an incompatible social system to village poverty, depriving the remote village of its most active manpower and overcrowding the urban and suburban village. Population growth adds to the problems created by population movement, for the twentieth-century introduction of European health and welfare services has drastically decreased the high mortality rate which had resulted from contact with European vices and diseases in the nineteenth century.

The historical demographic evidence in Samoa illustrates well some of the difficulties of arguing one way or the other from scanty or unreliable sources. For instance, the evidence for the population decline of the nineteenth century contained some estimates based on counts of wisps of smoke around a settlement. If only the mission records are used, the population of Samoa actually shows an increase in the nineteenth century if one mission figure (of which there was no record in the home society files) is omitted. In the early twentieth century births, deaths, and census registration were very haphazard, as many people knew little and cared less about these bureaucractic exercises.

The records concerning internal wage labor migration are not extensive either, for there were no formalities for going and living or working in town, though there is census and special survey material. But for most migrants the town of Apia was only a staging post for the shift to the more lucrative and prestigous watering places—American Samoa, Hawaii, the United States, and

New Zealand, where about 25% of all Samoans live. In all these cases the bureaucratic machine meticulously monitors the movement of the migrant and his wealth. For example, the New Zealand immigration authorities hold a file for every migrant, recording his complete demographic background, including such information as the location of all his relatives and the number of rooms in his house. Perhaps the most interesting statistic of all to emerge from this record, belittling the pessimistic view of migrant labor, is the large amount of money sent back by these migrants. In some villages and families, the migrant is the most important source of wealth. In addition, chain migration is common, the first settler in the new land bringing out and giving opportunities to relatives. Wealth and opportunity is further shared by the frequent trips Samoan migrants make home, to which many migrants claim they will retire. Samoan migration, like Samoan cash cropping and entrepreneurial activity, functions essentially within, and is supported by, the traditional social structure.

Conclusion

In building up the case for the positive role of traditional institutions in economic development in Samoa, historical documents and analytical methods played an important part; and this usefulness was achieved despite major drawbacks in the Samoan historical record. The record initially concerns a nonliterate people for which much important local material is preserved orally. Until recently, there has been little organized archival activity in the islands. Finally, the research topic was concerned with the economic activities of rural people, of little political interest, removed from urban centers and record repositories. Anthropologists and sociologists working in societies with a longer literate and archival tradition, or on issues of political interest and sensitivity, would have a larger harvest to reap.

Further Reading

A full report on this particular case study can be read in *Tradition and Economic Progress in Samoa* (Pitt 1970). Substantivist views have been collected by Dalton (1966), while Firth (1967) and Cook (1966) provide useful discussions. Students should read Max Weber's famous book *The Protestant Ethic and the Spirit of Capitalism* (1930). Two recent selections cover most of the debate on the historical and sociological aspects of the Weber thesis (Green 1959, S. N. Eisenstadt 1968), while a recent rebuttal is provided by Samuelson (1961). Sociological aspects of underdevelopment are discussed by Hoselitz (1960), while Ness (1970) offers the opinions of economists and sociologists on the question. Economist W. A. Lewis (1955) makes a most lucid statement. Smelser and Lipset (1966) are concerned with mobility. Two approaches from social psychology are those of Hagen (1962) and McClelland (1961). Excellent case studies of economic development have been written by anthropologists Belshaw (1964),

Geetz (1963), Nash (1965), and Salisbury (1962). Firth and Yamey (1964) have compiled useful material on the role of capital, savings and credit.

On Samoa itself there are useful missionary source materials, particularly the works of Turner (1861, 1884) and Stair (1897). Kramer (1902) provides a very detailed, if somewhat unreliable, account of traditional life. Mead (1930) offers a standard ethnographical source. Keesing (1934) has written an overview of social change, while Davidson (1967) provides a useful history. Stanner (1949) provides perceptive comments on development. Keesing and Keesing (1956) deal with elite communication, while Cumberland and Fox (1963) describe the agricultural system.

The student should go further and examine the sociological or anthropological uses of other kinds of models in a historical context. From this large literature the following can be recommended. In the political field, there are the works of Cohn and Singer (1968), Barnes (1967), Jones (1963), and M. G. Smith (1960). Firth (1929), Smelser (1959), and Geertz (1963) discuss economic models. Evans-Pritchard (1949), K. T. Erikson (1966), Worsley (1957), and Martin (1967) present valuable models in the field of religion. A specific thesis, Turner on the Frontier, has recently been discussed by sociologists and historians (Hofstadter and Lipset 1968). Further references are listed in the second half of the section Further Reading in Chapter 1 and in Handlin's guide (Handlin *et al.* 1966).

Conclusion

EVEN WHEN the historical documents have been located, collected, sorted, and analyzed, the job of historical research has only begun. The evidence from the documents now has to be utilized in the cut and thrust of argument and the web of exposition. The problems involved here would require another volume. However, if the research worker has carefully collected and collated his evidence, the job of integrating historical data with firsthand fieldwork or survey material can be undertaken with confidence.

6

Problems and Questions

THE PURPOSE of this final section is to set out for students and instructors a selection of questions and problems on the topics we have discussed in previous chapters. These questions are not intended to be comprehensive or of uniform difficulty. The main object is simply to stimulate further discussion and interest.

Chapter 1

1. Take any anthropological or sociological monograph which does not utilize historical data significantly and indicate the uses to which historical data might have been put.

2. Outline the ways in which ethnohistorians have used historical data.

3. Critically evaluate the structural–functionalist objections to historical perspectives.

4. Outline the obstacles to increasing links between history and cultural anthropology or sociology.

5. Why have many historians been reluctant to work on contemporary societies?

6. How would a "traditional" historian have dealt with any one of the topics in the Case Studies in Cultural Anthropology series, or any other relevant, contemporary problem in sociology or anthropology?

7. Present and evaluate the arguments that have been put forward to justify the concentration in historical studies on seeing events and situations as unique phenomena.

8. Compare and contrast the development of theories of history in Europe and North America.

9. Why have historians been most concerned with political studies?

10. Take any historical monograph and indicate the ways in which either a cultural anthropologist or a sociologist would have approached the problem.

11. Compare and contrast the interests of sociologists and cultural anthropologists in historical data.

12. How far do you think the professional institutional environment of either sociology or anthropology limits interest in historical models?

13. What historical training should an anthropologist or sociologist receive during his university training?

14. How useful for cultural anthropologists are the historical models found in other branches of anthropology, particularly archeology?

15. What future do you predict for relations between history and the social sciences?

Chapters 2 and 3

16. Outline a program of historical research for yourself, and name the likely documentary sources of information.

17. Describe and analyze the differential reliability of administration and mission sources in colonial areas.

18. Put yourself in the shoes of one of the following and produce the required document: (a) an explorer visiting a previously unexplored territory and describing the people he meets; (b) a missionary reporting to his home society or superior on the process of conversion in his area; (c) a trader writing a diary of his daily life in the village; (d) an immigrant to the United States writing a letter back to his home village in Europe.

19. Go through your own home and catalog the kinds of documentary materials which might be of use to a future historical researcher.

20. List the essential differences between verbal and nonverbal documents.

21. Examine from a sociological viewpoint the rituals and conventions involved in public archive use.

Chapter 4

22. From a source such as newspapers find two or more different accounts of the same event. Discuss and account for the differences of fact or emphasis which occur.

23. Examine, with examples, the contexts which favor accurate reporting of events.

24. Point out the ways in which facts can differ from statements about facts.

25. Write brief accounts of events in which you participated; (a) today, (b) yesterday, (c) last week, (d) some months ago, and (e) some years ago. Critically evaluate the nature of your own reporting.

26. Under what circumstances are features, events, and so forth not noticed adequately in an observation situation?

27. Discuss examples from the sociological or anthropological literature of cases where the author's subjectivity greatly influenced his (or her) research methods or interpretation.

28. Compare and contrast bias and error.

29. Critically evaluate the usefulness of methods of corroboration.

30. What are the limits on the use of inferential methods?

31. Outline possible applications for content analysis in cultural anthropology or sociology.

32. Outline and explain the different meanings that have been given at different times in history to any important concept which has had a wide range of semantic meaning (for example, democracy, freedom, property, or race).

33. Compare and contrast the methods to be used in translating from a foreign language and interpreting from a historical document.

34. Is it useful to talk about degrees of causation (such as Aristotelian efficient, formal, final, or critical causes) in the interpretation of historical evidence?

35. What is meant by the economic interpretation of history?

36. Examine the role of individual actions in any historical event with which you are familiar.

37. Examine the uses of the concept of causation in either cultural anthropology or sociology.

38. Do you think "accident" theories of history could have any application in anthropology or sociology?

39. What are the uses of oral history in historical interpretation?

40. Compare and contrast history and myth.

References

ABRAMS, M., 1968, Some Measurements of Social Satisfaction in Britain. In *Social Stratification*, J. A. Jackson (ed.). London: Cambridge.

ACOSTA, J. DE., 1880, *The Natural and Moral History of the Indies*. 2 vols. London: Hakluyt Society.

ADRIOT, J., 1961, *Guide to United States Government Statistics*. Arlington, Va.: Documents Index.

ANDERSON, R. T., 1963, *Changing Kinship in Europe*. Kroeber Anthropological Papers, No. 28. Berkeley, Calif.: Kroeber Anthropological Society.

ANDERSON, R. T., and B. G. ANDERSON, 1965, *Bus Stop for Paris: The Transformation of a French Village*. New York: Doubleday.

ARONSON, S. H., 1969, Obstacles to a Rapprochement between History and Sociology: A Sociologist's View. In *Interdisciplinary Relationships in the Social Sciences*, M. Sherif and C. W. Sherif (eds.). London: Aldine, pp. 292–304.

BAILEY, F. G., 1960, *Tribe, Caste, and Nation*. Manchester: Manchester University Press.

BALANDIER, G., 1951, *La Situation Coloniale: Approche Theorique*. Cahiers Internationaux de Sociologie, vol. XI, pp. 44–79.

———, 1968, *Daily Life in the Kingdom of the Kongo*. London: Allen.

BARNES, H. E., 1961, *A History of Historical Writing*. New York: Dover.

BARNES, J. A., 1967, *Politics in a Changing Society: A Political History of the Fort Jameson Ngoni*. Manchester: Manchester University Press.

BARRACLOUGH, G., 1964, *An Introduction to Contemporary History*. London: Watts.

BARROW, J. G., 1955, *A Bibliography of Bibliographies in Religion*. Ann Arbor, Mich.: Edwards.

BARZUN, J., and H. GRAFF, 1957, *The Modern Researcher*. New York: Harcourt.

BEAGLEHOLE, J. C., 1955, *The Journals of Captain James Cook*. London: Cambridge University Press for the Hakluyt Society.

BEALS, A. R., G. SPINDLER, and L. SPINDLER, 1967, *Culture in Process*. New York: Holt, Rinehart and Winston, Inc.

BEIDELMAN, T. O., 1959, *A Comparative Analysis of the Jajmani System*. Association of Asian Studies Monographs. Locust Valley, N.Y.: AAS.

BELSHAW, C. S., 1964, *Under the Ivi Tree*. London: Routledge.

BENNETT, H. S., 1952, *English Books and Readers, 1475–1557*. London: Cambridge.

BERELSON, B., 1952, *Content Analysis in Communication Research*. Glencoe, Ill.: Free Press.

BERLIN, I., 1955, *Historical Inevitability*. New York: Oxford.

BESANÇON, A., 1967, *Le Tsarevitch Immolé*. Paris: Plon.

BESTERMAN, T., 1964–1966. *A World Bibliography of Bibliographies*. Lausanne: Societas Bibliographica.

BEYLE, M. H. [Stendhal], 1962, *Memoirs of a Tourist*. Translated by Allan Seager. Evanston, Ill.: Northwestern University Press.

BIBLIOTHECA MISSIONUM, 1916–. Münster: Internationales Institute für Missionswissen-schaffliche Forschung.

BLOCH, M., 1954, *The Historian's Craft*. Manchester: Manchester University Press.

———, 1961, *Feudal Society*. London: Routledge.

———, 1966, *French Rural History: An Essay on its Basic Characteristics*. London: Routledge.

BOHANNAN, L., 1952, A Genealogical Charter. *Africa* 22: 301–315.

BORDIN, R. B., and R. M. WARNER, 1966, *The Modern Manuscript Library*. New York: Scarecrow.

BOSWELL, J., 1923, *Journal of a Tour to Corsica*. Edited by S. C. Roberts. London: Cambridge.

———, 1955, *Boswell on the Grand Tour: Italy, Corsica and France, 1765–1766*. Edited by F. Brady and F. A. Pottle. New York: McGraw-Hill.

BOWLES, E. (ed.), 1967, *Computers in Humanistic Research*. Englewood Cliffs, N.J.: Prentice-Hall.

BRAIMAH, J. A., and J. R. GOODY, 1967, *Salaga: The Struggle for Power*. London: Longmans.

BRIDENBAUGH, C., 1963, The Great Mutation. *American Historical Review* 68: 315–331.

BROWN, E. S., 1950, *Manual of Government Publications*. New York: Appleton.

BROWN, L. A., 1949, *The Story of Maps*. Boston: Little Brown.

BURSTON, W. H., and D. THOMPSON, 1967, *Studies in the Nature and Teaching of History*. London: Routledge.

CAHNMAN, W. J., and A. BOSKOFF (eds.), 1964, *Sociology and History: Theory and Research*. New York: Free Press.

CALLAWAY, H., 1868–1870, *The Religious System of the Amazulu*. Natal: J. A. Blair.

CANTOR, N., 1968, Medieval Historiography as Modern Political and Social Thought. *Journal of Contemporary History* 3: 55–73.

CANTRIL, H., 1947, *Gauging Public Opinion*. Princeton, N.J.: Princeton University Press.

CAREY, G. V., 1951, *Making an Index*. London: Cambridge.

CARR, E. H., 1964, *What Is History?* Hamondsworth: Penguin.

CARRASCO, P., 1959, *Land and Polity in Tibet*. Seattle: University of Washington Press.

CARSON, P., 1965, *Materials for West African History in the Archives of Belgium and Holland*. London: Athlone Press.

———, 1968, *Materials for West African History in French Archives*. London: Athlone Press.

CATO, A. C., 1951, Malolo Island and Viseisei Village, Western Fiji. *Oceania* 22: 101–115.

CHARLEVOIX, P. F. X. DE, 1900, *History and General Description of New France*. New York: Harper.

CLAGHORN, K. H., 1923, *The Immigrant's Day in Court*. New York: Harper & Row.

COCHRAN, T. C., 1964, *The Inner Revolution: Essays on the Social Sciences in History*. New York: Harper & Row.

CODRINGTON, R. H., 1891, *The Melanesians: Studies in Their Anthropology and Folklore*. Oxford: Clarendon Press.

COHEN, A., 1965, *Arab Border Villages in Israel*. Manchester: Manchester University Press.

COHEN, P. S., 1968, *Modern Social Theory*. London: Heinemann.

COHN, B. S., 1962, An Anthropologist among the Historians: A Field Study. *South Atlantic Quarterly* 61, pt. 1: 13–28.

COHN, B. S., and M. SINGER, 1968, *Structure and Change in Indian Society*. Viking Publications in Anthropology, No. 47. New York: Viking.

COLLIER, J., 1967, *Visual Anthropology*. New York: Holt, Rinehart and Winston, Inc.

COLLINGWOOD, R., 1945, *The Idea of History*. New York: Oxford University Press.

COLLOQUE DE L'ÉCOLE NORMALE SUPERIEURE, 1967, *L'Histoire Sociale: Sources et Methodes*. Paris: Presses Universitaires de France.

COMAN, E. T., 1964, *Sources of Business Information*. Los Angeles: University of California Press.

COOK, S., 1966, The Obsolete "Anti-Market" Mentality. *American Anthropologist* 68: 323–345.

COSER, L., 1964, *The Functions of Social Conflict*. New York: Free Press.

COUNCIL OF SOCIAL SCIENCE DATA ARCHIVES, 1967, *Social Science Data Archives in the United States*. New York: CSSDA.

CROCOMBE, R., 1964, *Land Tenure in the Cook Islands*. London: Oxford.

CUMBERLAND, K. B., and J. W. FOX (eds.), 1962, *Western Samoa*. Wellington: Whitcombe and Tombs.

CUNNISON, I., 1959, *The Luapala Peoples of Northern Rhodesia: Custom and History in Tribal Politics*. Manchester: Manchester University Press.

CURTIN, P. (ed.), 1967, *Africa Remembered*. Madison: University of Wisconsin Press.

DAEDALUS, 1968, *Historical Population Studies*, vol. 97, no. 2.

DAHRENDORF, R., 1959, *Class and Conflict*. Stanford, Calif.: Stanford University Press.

DALTON, G., 1966, *Tribal and Peasant Economies*. New York: American Museum of Natural History.

DAVIDSON, J. W., 1967, *Samoa mo Samoa*. London: Oxford.

DEXTER, L. A., and D. M. WHITE (eds.), 1964, *People, Society, and Mass Communications*. New York: Free Press.

DIAZ, N. M., 1966, *Tonala: Conservatism, Responsibility and Authority in a Mexican Town*. Berkeley: University of California Press.

DOANE, G. H., 1960, *Searching for Your Ancestors: The How and Why of Genealogy*. 3d ed. Minneapolis: University of Minnesota Press.

DOBRITZHOFER, M., 1822, *An Account of the Abipones, an Equestrian People of Paraguay*. London: J. Murray.

DOLLAR, C., and R. JENSEN, 1970, *Quantitative Approaches in Historical Analysis*. New York: Holt, Rinehart and Winston, Inc.

DOVRING, F., 1960, *History As a Social Science: An Essay on the Nature and Purpose of Historical Studies*. The Hague: Nijhoff.

DOW, E. W., 1924, *Principles of a Note-System for Historical Studies*. New York: Appleton.

DOWNS, R. B., and F. B. JENKINS, 1967, *Bibliography*. Urbana, Ill.: University of Illinois Press.

DUBOIS, J. A., 1817, *Description of the Character, Manners, and Customs of the People of India, and of Their Institutions, Religious and Civil*. London: Longmans.

DUMAS, A., 1953, *From Paris to Cadiz*. Translated and edited by A. E. Murch. London: Owen.

———, 1958, *Travels in Switzerland*. Translated by R. W. Plummer and A. C. Bell. London: Owen.

DUNN, E., and S. DUNN, 1967, *The Peasants of Central Russia*. New York: Holt, Rinehart and Winston, Inc.

DURKHEIM, E., 1951, *Suicide*. New York: Free Press.

———, 1961, *The Elementary Forms of Religious Life*. New York: Crowell-Collier-Macmillan.

EDMONDS, W. D., 1936, How You Begin a Novel. *Atlantic Monthly* 158: 189.

EGGAN, F., 1966, *The American Indian.* Chicago: Aldine.

EISENSTADT, A. D. (ed.), 1966, *The Craft of American History.* New York: Harper & Row.

EISENSTADT, S. N., 1968, *The Protestant Ethic and Modernization.* New York: Basic Books.

ELLIS, W., 1828, *Narrative of a Tour Through Hawaii, or Whyhee, with Remarks on the History, Traditions, Manners, Customs, and Language of the Inhabitants of the Sandwich Islands.* London: Fisher & Jackson.

———, 1839–1842, *Polynesian Researches, during a Residence of Nearly Eight Years in the Society and Sandwich Islands.* 4 vols. London: Fisher & Jackson.

ELTON, G. R., 1967, *The Practice of History.* New York: Crowell.

ENCOUNTER, 1969, The Uses and Abuses of History. London: *Encounter* (October).

ERIKSON, E. H., 1959, *Young Man Luther: A Study in Psychoanalysis and History.* London: Faber.

ERIKSON, K. T., 1966, *Wayward Puritans.* New York: Wiley.

EVANS-PRITCHARD, E. E., 1949, *The Sanusi of Cyrenaica.* London: Oxford.

———, 1961, *Anthropology and History.* Manchester: Manchester University Press.

EWERS, J. C., 1955, *The Horse in Blackfoot Indian Culture, with Comparative Material from Other Western Tribes.* Bureau of American Ethnology Bulletin No. 159, Washington, D.C.: BAE.

FENTON, W. N., 1952, The Training of Historical Ethnologists in America. *American Anthropologist* 54: 328–339.

FIRTH, R., 1929, *Primitive Economics of the New Zealand Maori.* London: Routledge.

———, 1959, *Social Change in Tikopia.* London: G. Allen.

FIRTH, R. (ed)., 1967, *Themes in Economic Anthropology.* London: Tavistock.

FIRTH, R., and B. S. YAMEY (eds.), 1964, *Capital Savings and Credit in Peasant Society.* London: G. Allen.

FORD, C. D., 1956, *Selected Annotated Bibliography of Tropical Africa.* London: International African Institute.

FORD, P., and F. FORD, 1955, *A Guide to Parliamentary Papers.* Oxford: Blackwell.

FORTES, M., 1949, Time and Social Structure. In *Social Structure: Studies Presented to A. R. Radcliffe-Brown.* London: Oxford.

———, 1958, *Introduction: The Development Cycle in Domestic Groups,* J. R. Goody (ed.). Cambridge Papers in Social Anthropology, No. 1 New York: Cambridge.

FRANCE, P., 1969, *The Charter of the Land.* London: Oxford.

FREEMAN, J. F., and M. D. SMITH, 1966, *A Guide to Manuscripts Relating to the American Indian in the Library of the American Philosophical Society.* American Philosophical Society Memoir 65. Philadelphia: APS.

FÜRER-HAIMENDORF, E. VON, 1958–1964, *An Anthropological Bibliography of South Asia.* Paris: Mouton.

GALBRAITH, V. H., 1952, *Introduction to the Use of the Public Records.* London: Oxford.

GARRAGHAN, G. J., and J. DELANGLEZ (eds.), 1946, *A Guide to Historical Method.* New York: Fordham University Press.

GEERTZ, C., 1963, *Agricultural Involution.* Berkeley: University of California Press.

GEORGE, H. B., 1909, *Historical Evidence.* Oxford: Clarendon Press.

GEYL, P., 1955, *Use and Abuse of History.* New Haven, Conn.: Yale University Press.

GHOSE, S., 1963, *Archives in India.* Calcutta: Mukhopadhyay.

GIBBON, E., 1961, *Gibbon's Journey from Geneva to Rome.* Edited by George A. Bonnard. London: Nelson.

GILL, W. W., 1876, *Life in the Southern Isles; or Scenes and Incidents in the South Pacific and New Guinea.* London: Religious Tract Society.

GLUCKMAN, M., 1947, Malinowski's "Functional" Analysis of Social Change. *Africa* 17: 106–121.

————, 1968, The Utility of the Equilibrium Model in the Study of Social Change. *American Anthropologist* 70: 219–238.

GOLDSCHMIDT, W., 1966, *Comparative Functionalism.* Cambridge: Cambridge University Press.

GOLDSTEIN, K. S., 1964, *A Guide for Fieldworkers in Folklore.* Hartboro, Pa.: Folklore Associates (published for the American Folklore Society).

GOMEZ CANEDO, L., 1961, *Los archivos de la historia de America.* Mexico City: Instituto Panamericano de Geografia e Historia.

GOTTSCHALK, L., C. KLUCKHOHN, and R. ANGELL, 1945, *The Use of Personal Documents in History, Anthropology, and Sociology.* New York: Social Science Research Council.

GOTTSCHALK, L. (ed.), 1963, *Generalization in the Writing of History.* Chicago: University of Chicago Press.

————, 1969, *Understanding History.* New York: Knopf.

GOUGH, K., 1952, Changing Kinship Usages in the Setting of Political and Economic Change among the Nayars of Malabar. *Journal of the Royal Anthropological Institute* 82: 71–87.

GOULDNER, A. W., 1956, Some Observations on Systematic Theory, 1945–1955. In *Sociology in the United States of America.* Paris: UNESCO.

GRANET, M., 1930, *Chinese Civilization.* London: K. Paul, Trench, Trubner & Coy.

GRAS, N. W. B., 1930, *The Economic and Social History of an English Village.* Cambridge, Mass.: Harvard University Press.

GRAY, R., and D. CHAMBERS, 1965, *Materials for West African History in Italian Archives.* London: Athlone Press.

GREEN, R. W., 1959, *Protestantism and Capitalism.* Boston: Heath.

GUDSCHINSKY, S. C., 1967, *How to Learn an Unwritten Language.* New York: Holt, Rinehart and Winston, Inc.

GULLICK, J. M., 1958, *Indigenous Political Systems of Western Malaya,* L.S.E. Monographs in Social Anthropology No. 17, London: Athlone.

GUNNERSON, J. H., 1957, *A Survey of Ethnohistoric Sources.* Kroeber Anthropological Society Papers, No. 16, pp. 39–65. Berkeley, Calif.: Kroeber Anthropological Society.

HAGEN, E. E., 1962, *On the Theory of Social Change.* Homewood, Ill.: The Dorsey Press.

HALE, R. W., 1961, *Guide to Photocopied Historical Materials in the United States and Canada.* Ithaca, N.Y.: Cornell University Press.

HALPERIN, W. (ed.), 1960, *Some Twentieth-Century Historians: Essays on Eminent Europeans.* Chicago: University of Chicago Press.

HALPERN, B., 1957, History, Sociology, and Contemporary Area Studies, *American Journal of Sociology* 63: 1–10.

HAMER, P. M. (ed.), 1961, *A Guide to Archives and Manuscripts in the United States.* New Haven, Conn.: Yale University Press.

HANDLIN, O., *et al.*, 1966, *Harvard Guide to American History.* Cambridge, Mass.: Belknap.

HARRIS, M., 1968, *The Rise of Anthropological Theory.* New York: Crowell.

HENDERSON, G. P., 1957 *et seq., Reference Manual of Directories.* London: Jones and Evans.

HEPWORTH, P., 1966, *How to Find Out in History.* New York: Pergamon.

HEWITT, A. R., 1957, *Guide to Resources for Commonwealth Studies.* London: Press.

————, 1960, *Union List of Commonwealth Newspapers in London, Oxford, and Cambridge.* London: Athlone Press.

HICKERSON, H., 1962, *The Southwestern Chippewa: An Ethnohistoric Study.* American Anthropological Association Memoir No. 92. Menasha, Wis.: AAA.

————, 1970, *The Chippewa and Their Neighbors.* New York: Holt, Rinehart and Winston, Inc.

HIGHAM, J., L. KRIEGER, and F. GILBERT, 1965, *History*. Englewood Cliffs, N.J.: Prentice-Hall.

HISTORICAL MANUSCRIPTS COMMISSION, 1956, *Record Depositories in Great Britain*. London: H. M. Stationery Office.

HOCKETT, H. C., 1955, *The Critical Method in Historical Research and Writing*. New York: Crowell-Collier-Macmillan.

HOFSTADTER, R., and S. M. LIPSET, 1968, *Turner and the Sociology of the Frontier*. New York: Basic Books.

HOMANS, G. C., 1960, *English Villagers of the Thirteenth Century*. New York: Russell & Russell.

HOMANS, G. C., and D. M. SCHNEIDER, 1955, *Marriage, Authority, and Final Causes*. New York: Free Press.

HOSELITZ, B., 1960, *Sociological Aspects of Economic Growth*. New York: Free Press.

HOSKINS, W. G., 1959, *Local History in England*. London: Longmans.

————, 1965, *The Midland Peasant: The Economic and Social History of a Leicestershire Village*. London: Collier-Macmillan, Ltd.

HUC, E. R., 1852, *Recollections of a Journey through Tartary, Tibet, and China, During the Years 1844, 1845, & 1846*. New York: Appleton.

————, 1855, *The Chinese Empire*. London: Longmans.

HUGHES, H. S., 1964, *History as Art and as a Science*. New York: Harper & Row.

INKELES, A., and K. GEIGER, 1961, *Soviet Society*. Boston: Houghton Mifflin.

INTERNATIONAL JOURNAL OF THE SOCIAL SCIENCES, 1965, *History and Social Science*, vol. 17 no. 4.

JANOWITZ, M., and W. E. DAUGHERTY (eds.), 1958, *A Psychological Warfare Casebook*. Baltimore: The Johns Hopkins Press.

JARVIE, I. C., 1964, *The Revolution in Anthropology*. London: Routledge.

JENKINSON, H., 1965, *A Manual of Archive Administration*. London: Percy, Lund, Humphries & Coy.

JENNINGS, P., 1968, *The Living Village*. London: Hodder & Stoughton.

The Jesuit Relations and Allied Documents, 1896–1901, *Travels and Explorations of the Jesuit Missionaries in New France, 1610–1791*. 73 vols. Cleveland: Burrows.

JONES, G. I., 1963, *The Trading States of the Oil Rivers: A Study of Political Development in Eastern Nigeria*. London: Oxford.

JOURNAL OF CONTEMPORARY HISTORY, 1968, Reappraisals: A New Look at History. *Journal of Contemporary History* 3: 2.

JUNOD, H. A., 1912–1913, *The Life of a South African Tribe (The Thonga)*. London: D. Nutt.

KARTINI, R. A., 1964, *Letters of a Javanese Princess*. Edited and with an introduction by H. Geertz. New York: Norton.

KEESING, F. M., 1934, *Modern Samoa*. London: G. Allen.

————, 1953, *Culture Change*. Stanford, Calif.: Stanford University Press.

————, 1962, *The Ethnohistory of Northern Luzon*. Stanford, Calif.: Stanford University Press.

KEESING, F. M., and M. KEESING, 1956, *Elite Communication in Samoa*. Stanford, Calif.: Stanford University Press.

KENT, S., 1954, *Writing History*. New York: Appleton.

KITSON, CLARK, G., 1967, *The Critical Historian*, London: Heinemann.

KRAMER, A., 1902, *Die Samoa Inseln*. Stuttgart: Naegle.

KROEBER, A., 1935, History and Science in Anthropology. *American Anthropologist* 37: 539–570.

————, 1963, *An Anthropologist Looks at History*. Berkeley: University of California Press.

KRUG, M., 1967, *History and the Social Sciences*. Waltham, Mass.: Blaisdell.

LAFITAU, J. F., 1839, *Moeurs, Coutumes et Religions des Sauvages Americains*. Paris: Perisse.

LAGUNA, F. DE, 1960, *The Story of a Tlingit Community: A Problem in the Relationship between Archeological, Ethnological, and Historical Methods.* Bureau of American Ethnology Bulletin No. 172. Washington, D.C.: BAE.

LANCASTER, L., 1958, Kinship in Anglo-Saxon Society. *British Journal of Sociology* 9: 230–250, 359–377.

LANGLOIS, C. V., and C. SEIGNOBOS, 1898, *Introduction to the Study of History.* London: Duckworth.

LANTZ, H. R., M. BRITTON, R. SCHMITT, and E. C. SNYDER, 1968, Preindustrial Patterns in the Colonial Family in America: A Content Analysis of Colonial Magazines. *American Sociological Review* 33, no. 3: 413–426.

LARSON, H. M., 1948, *Guide to Business History.* New York: Cambridge.

LASLETT, P., 1965, *The World We Have Lost.* London: Methuen.

LEACH, E. R., 1964, *Political Systems of Highland Burma.* Boston: Beacon.

LEAR, E., 1966, *Edward Lear in Corsica.* London: Kimber.

LEFF, G., 1969, *History and Social Theory.* London: Merlin Press.

LESCARBOT, M., 1907–1914, *The History of New France.* Toronto: The Champlain Society.

LEVI-STRAUSS, C., 1970, *The Raw and the Cooked.* London: Cape.

LEWIS, I. M., 1966, Spirit Possession and Deprivation Cults. *Man* NS1: 307–129.

———, (ed.), 1968, *History and Social Anthropology.* London: Tavistock.

LEWIS, O., 1951, *Life in a Mexican Village: Tepoztlán Restudied.* Urbana, Ill.: University of Illinois Press.

———, 1959, *Five Families.* New York: Basic Books.

LEWIS, W. A., 1955, *The Theory of Economic Growth.* London: G. Allen.

LIPSET, S. M., and R. HOFSTADTER (eds.), 1968, *Sociology and History: Methods.* New York: Basic Books.

LIVINGSTONE, D., 1963, *African Journal: 1853–1856.* London: Chatto.

LLOYD, P. (ed.), 1966, *The New Elites of Tropical Africa.* London: Oxford.

LONDON BIBLIOGRAPHY OF THE SOCIAL SCIENCES, 1931–1968, 21 vols. London: London School of Economics.

LONDON *Times Literary Supplement*, Special History Number, April 7, 1966.

LOPREATO, J., 1967, *Peasants No More.* San Francisco: Chandler Publishing Company.

LOUNSBURY, F. G., 1964, The Latin Kinship System and Its Relationship to Roman Social Organization. Paper read at the Seventh International Congress in Anthropological and Ethnological Sciences, Moscow, 1964. In press (*Proceedings of the Congress*).

McCALL, D. F., 1964, *Africa in Time Perspective: A Discussion of Historical Reconstruction from Unwritten Sources.* Boston: Boston University Press.

McCLELLAND, D. C., 1961, *The Achieving Society.* Princetown, N.J.: Van Nostrand.

MacIVER, R. M., 1942, *Social Causation.* Boston: Ginn.

MACK, R. W., 1969, Theoretical and Substantive Biases in Sociological Research. In *Interdisciplinary Relationships in the Social Sciences.* M. Sherif and C. W. Sherif (eds.), Chicago: Aldine, pp. 52–64.

MALINOWSKI, B., 1945, *Dynamics of Culture Change.* New Haven, Conn.: Yale University Press.

MARCHANT, L. R., 1966, *A Guide to the Archives and Records of Protestant Christian Missions from the British Isles to China.* Perth: University of Western Australia Press.

MARSH, R. M., 1967, *Comparative Sociology.* New York: Harcourt Brace.

MARTIN, D., 1967, *A Sociology of English Religion.* London: SCM Press.

MEAD, M., 1930, *Social Organization of Manua*, Honolulu: B. P. Bishop Museum Bulletin No. 76.

———, 1951, Anthropologist and Historian: Their Common Problems. *American Quarterly* 3 (Spring): 3–13.

MEHTA, V., 1963, *Fly and the Fly Bottle.* London: Weidenfeld & Nicholson.

MEYERHOFF, H., 1959, *The Philosophy of History in our Time.* New York: Doubleday.

MIDDLETON, J., 1960, *Lugbara Religion.* London: Oxford.

MORISON, S. E., 1951, Faith of a Historian. *American Historical Review* 66: 261–275.

MURPHY, R. F., 1967, Cultural Change. *Biennial Review of Anthropology* 1967: 1–46.

MURRA, J. (ed.), 1967, *Iñigo Ortiz de Zúñiga: Visita de la Provincia de Leon de Huanuco en 1562.* Huánuco, Peru: Universidad Nacional Hermilio Valdizan.

NAKANE, C., 1967, *Kinship and Economic Organization in Rural Japan.* London: Athlone Press.

NASH, M., 1965, *The Golden Road to Modernity.* New York: Wiley.

NEEDHAM, R., 1962, *Structure and Sentiment.* Chicago: University of Chicago Press.

NESS, G. D., 1970, *The Sociology of Economic Development.* New York: Harper & Row.

NEVINS, A., 1962, *The Gateway to History.* New York: Doubleday.

NORTH, R. C., O. R. HOLSTI, M. G. ZANINOVICH, and D. A. ZINNES, 1963, *Content Analysis.* Evanston, Ill.: Northwestern University Press.

PARKER, D. D., 1944, *Local History.* New York: Social Science Research Council.

PENNIMAN, T. K., 1965, *A Hundred Years of Anthropology.* London: Duckworth.

PETERS, E., 1960, The Proliferation of Segments in the Lineage of the Bedouin of Cyrenaica. *Journal of the Royal Anthropological Institute* 90: 29–53.

PITT, D. C., 1970, *Tradition and Economic Progress in Samoa.* Oxford: Clarendon Press.

POLANYI, K., *et al.*, 1957, *Trade and Market in the Early Empires.* New York: Free Press.

POOL, I. DE S. (ed.), 1959, *Trends in Content Analysis.* Urbana, Ill.: University of Illinois Press.

POPPER, K., 1957, *The Poverty of Historicism.* London: Routledge.

POSTGATE, J. P., 1922, *Translation and Translations.* London: Bell.

POTTER, J., *et al.* (eds.), 1967, *Peasant Society.* Boston: Little, Brown.

RANKE, L. VON, 1824 *Zur Kritik Neuerer Geschichtschreiber, von Leopold Ranke; eine Beylaga zu Desselben Romanischen und Germanischen Geschichten.* Leipzig: G. Reimer.

REDFIELD, R., 1930, *Tepoztlán: A Mexican Village.* Chicago: The University of Chicago Press.

RILEY, M. W., 1963, *Sociological Research.* New York: Harcourt.

ROKKAN, S. (ed.), 1966, *Data Archives for the Social Sciences.* Paris: Mouton.

ROSCOE, J., 1911, *The Baganda: An Account of Their Native Customs and Beliefs.* London: Macmillan.

RUDÉ, G., 1958, *The Crowd in the French Revolution.* London: Oxford.

RYDER, A. F. C., 1965, *Materials for West African History in Portuguese Archives.* London: Athlone Press.

SALISBURY, R. F., 1962, *From Stone to Steel.* Melbourne: Cambridge University Press.

SAMARAN, C., 1961, *L'Histoire et ses Methodes.* Paris: Librairie Gallimard.

SAMUELSON, K., 1961, *Religion and Economic Action.* London: Heinemann.

SAVETH, E. (ed.), 1964, *American History and the Social Sciences.* New York: Free Press.

SCHAPERA, I., 1962, Should Anthropologists Be Historians? *Journal of the Royal Anthropological Institute* 92: 143–156.

SCHARER, H., 1963, *Ngaju Religion.* The Hague: Nijhoff.

SCHELLENBERG, T. R., 1965, *The Management of Archives.* New York: Columbia University Press.

SCHMIDT, W., 1926–1955, *Der Ursprung der Gottesidee.* 12 vols. Münster: Ascherdoff.

SEGAL, R., 1961, *Political Africa.* London: Stevens.

SHERIF, M., and C. W. SHERIF, 1969, *Interdisciplinary Relationships in the Social Sciences.* Chicago: Aldine.

SIEGEL, B. J. (ed.), *et al.*, 1959 et seq., *Biennial Review of Anthropology.* Stanford: Stanford University Press.

SIEGFRIED, A., 1951, *African Journey.* Translated by Edward Fitzgerald. London: Jonathan Cape.

SKINNER, G. W., 1957, *Chinese Society in Thailand.* Ithaca: Cornell University Press.

SMELSER, N. J., 1959, *Social Change in the Industrial Revolution.* London: Routledge.

SMELSER, N. J., and S. M. LIPSET, 1966, *Social Structure and Mobility in Economic Development.* London: Routledge.

SMITH, E. W., 1920, *The Ila-Speaking Peoples of Northern Rhodesia.* London: Macmillan.

———, 1927, *The Golden Stool: Some Aspects of the Conflict of Cultures in Africa.* London: Holborne.

SMITH, M. G., 1960, *Government in Zazzau: A Study of Government in the Hausa Chiefdom of Zaria in Northern Nigeria from 1800 to 1950.* London: Oxford.

———, 1962, History and Social Anthropology. *Journal of the Royal Anthropological Institute* 92: 73–85.

SMITH, R. J., 1962, Japanese Kinship Terminology: The History of a Nomenclature. *Ethnology* 1: 349–359.

SOCIAL SCIENCE RESEARCH COUNCIL, 1954, *The Social Sciences in Historical Study.* Social Science Research Council Bulletin No. 54. New York: SSRC.

SOROKIN, P. A., 1962, *Social and Cultural Dynamics.* New York: Bedminster Press.

SOUTHALL, A. (ed.), 1961, *Social Change in Modern Africa.* London: Oxford.

SOUTHWOLD, M., 1968, The History of a History: Royal Succession in Buganda. In *History and Social Anthropology,* I. Lewis (ed.), London: Tavistock.

SPICER, E. H. (ed)., 1961, *Perspectives in American Indian Culture Change.* Chicago: University of Chicago Press.

———, 1962, *Cycles of Conquest.* Tucson: University of Arizona Press.

STAIR, J. B., 1897, *Old Samoa.* London: Religious Tract Society.

STANNER, W. E. H., 1953, *The South Seas in Transition.* Sydney: Australasian Publishing Co.

STERN, F. (ed.), 1956, *The Varieties of History.* New York: Meridian.

STEVENSON, R. L., 1892, *A Footnote to History: Eight Years of Trouble in Samoa.* London: Cassells.

STEWARD, J. H., 1955, *Theory of Culture Change.* Urbana, Ill.: University of Illinois Press.

STOCKING, G., 1968, *Race, Culture, and Evolution.* New York: Free Press.

STREHLOW, C., 1907–1920. *Die Aranda: Und Loritja-stämme in Zentral Australien.* Frankfurt am Main: J. Baen.

STROUT, C., 1958, *The Pragmatic Revolt in American History: Carl Becker and Charles Beard.* New Haven, Conn.: Yale.

STURTEVANT, W. C., 1966, Anthropology, History, and Ethnohistory. *Ethnohistory* 13: 2–51.

SUSSMAN, L., 1963, *Dear F.D.R.* Totowa, N.J.: Bedminster.

TAYLOR, C. R., 1965, *A Pacific Bibliography.* London: Oxford.

THERNSTROM, S., 1964, *Poverty and Progress: Social Mobility in a Nineteenth-Century City.* Cambridge, Mass.: Harvard University Press.

THOMAS, K., 1963, History and Anthropology. *Past and Present* 24: 3–25.

THOMAS, W. I., and F. ZNANIECKI, 1958, *The Polish Peasant in Europe and America.* New York: Dover.

THOMSON, D., 1969, *The Aims of History.* London: Thames and Hudson.

THRUPP, S., 1957, History and Sociology: New Opportunities for Cooperation. *American Journal of Sociology* 63: 11–16.

TILLY, C., 1964, *The Vendée.* Cambridge, Mass.: Harvard University Press.

TOCQUEVILLE, A. C. H. M. C. DE, 1958, *Journeys to England and Ireland.* Translated by G. Lawrence and K. P. Mayer. Edited by J. P. Mayer. New Haven, Conn.: Yale University Press, Anchor Books.

———, 1960, *Journey to America*. Translated by G. Lawrence. Edited by J. P. Mayer. New Haven, Conn.: Yale University Press.

TRIGGER, B., 1969, *The Huron: Farmers of the North*. New York: Holt, Rinehart and Winston, Inc.

TURNER, G., 1861, *Nineteen Years in Polynesia: Missionary Life, Travels, and Researches in the Islands of the Pacific*. London: J. Snow.

———, 1884, *Samoa, a Hundred Years Ago and Long Before: Together with Notes on the Cults and Customs of Twenty-three Other Islands in the Pacific*. London: Macmillan.

VANN WOODWARD, C., 1968, History and the Third Culture. *Journal of Contemporary History* 3: 23–35.

VANSINA, J., 1965, *Oral Tradition*. London: Routledge.

VICKERY, B. C., 1961, *On Retrieval System Theory*. London: Butterworth.

VINCENT, J. M., 1911, *Historical Research*. New York: Holt, Rinehart and Winston, Inc.

WALLERSTEIN, I., 1966, *Social Change: The Colonial Situation*. New York: Wiley.

WALSH, W. H., 1951, *An Introduction to Philosophy of History*. London: Hutchinson's University Library.

WARE, C. (ed.), 1950, *The Cultural Approach to History*. New York: Columbia University Press.

WARNER, W. L., 1959, *The Living and the Dead*. New Haven, Conn.: Yale University Press.

WASSERMAN, P. (ed.), 1962 *et seq.*, *Statistics Sources*. Detroit: Gale Research.

WEBB, E. J., *et al.*, 1966, *Unobtrusive Measures*. Skokie, Ill.: Rand McNally.

WEBER, M., 1930, *The Protestant Ethic and the Spirit of Capitalism*. Translated by Talcott Parsons. London: G. Allen.

———, 1952, *The Religion of China*. Translated and edited by H. H. Gerth. New York: Free Press.

———, 1958, *The Religion of India*. Translated and edited by H. H. Gerth and D. Martindale. New York: Free Press.

WERTHEIM, W. F., 1964, The Sociological Approach. In *An Introduction to Indonesian Historiography*, Mohammad Ali, G. J. Resink, and G. M. Kahin (eds.). Ithaca, N.Y.: Cornell University Press.

WHITE, M., 1965, *Foundations of Historical Knowledge*. New York: Harper & Row.

WHYTE, W. F., 1969, *Organizational Behavior*. Homewood, Ill.: The Dorsey Press.

WILKES, C., 1847, *Narrative of the United States Exploring Expedition During the Years 1838, 1839*, 5 vols. Philadelphia.

WILSON, G., 1939, *The Constitution of Ngonda*. Rhodes Livingstone Institute Paper No. 3. London: Oxford.

WINCHELL, C. M. (ed.), 1967, *Guide to Reference Books*. Chicago: American Library Association.

WISH, H., 1960, *The American Historian*. New York: Oxford.

WOOD GRAY *et al.*, 1964, *Historian's Handbook*. Boston: Houghton Mifflin.

WOODS, R. A., 1898, *The City Wilderness*. Boston: Houghton Mifflin.

WORSLEY, P., 1957, *The Trumpet Shall Sound*. London: McGibbon, Kee.

WRIGHT, G., 1964, *Rural Revolution in France*. Stanford, Calif.: Stanford University Press.

YOE, S., 1963, *The Burman: His Life and Notions*. New York: Norton.

YOUNG, A., 1929, *Travels in France during the Years 1787, 1788, 1789*. Cambridge: Cambridge University Press.

ZUBRZYCKI, J., 1964, *Settlers of the La Trobe Valley*. Canberra: Australian National University Press.